THE SMASHING
Idea Book:

FROM INSPIRATION TO APPLICATION

THE SMASHING
Idea Book:
FROM INSPIRATION TO APPLICATION

Cameron Chapman

A John Wiley and Sons, Ltd, Publication

PUBLISHER'S ACKNOWLEDGEMENTS

Some of the people who helped bring this book to market include the following:

Editorial and Production
VP Consumer and Technology Publishing Director: Michelle Leete
Associate Director–Book Content Management: Martin Tribe
Associate Publisher: Chris Webb
Publishing Assistant: Ellie Scott
Development Editor: Kezia Endsley
Copy Editor: Kezia Endsley
Technical Editor: Alexander Charchar
Editorial Manager: Jodi Jensen
Senior Project Editor: Sara Shlaer
Editorial Assistant: Leslie Saxman

Marketing
Senior Marketing Manager: Louise Breinholt
Marketing Executive: Kate Parrett

Composition Services
Compositor: Erin Zeltner
Proofreader: Susan Hobbs
Indexer: Potomac Indexing, LLC

About the Author

CAMERON CHAPMAN is a largely self-taught designer with a formal education in interior design and a practical background in both web and print design, gained primarily while working for a national real estate magazine. She has written about design and social media for a number of leading blogs, including *Smashing Magazine, Mashable, Six Revisions,* and *Webdesigner Depot.*

Cameron has been an editor at *Smashing Magazine* and for the Tuts+ Network. Currently, she splits her time between writing about design and actually designing, with a focus on the former in recent years.

Author's Acknowledgments

FIRST, THANK YOU to Kezia Endsley, Chris Webb, Ellie Scott, Sara Shlaer, Leslie Saxman, Alex Charchar, and everyone else at Wiley who made this book possible. Thank you to Vitaly Friedman, Sven Lennartz, and everyone else at *Smashing Magazine* for being fantastic people to work for and with. Thank you to Pete Cashmore for hiring a mostly-unknown environmental blogger to write regularly for *Mashable*, which gave me the initial credibility to get every other blogging job I've had. And a huge thank you to my husband and fellow designer, Mike Moffit, for getting me started with graphic and web design, and for helping me figure out coding problems whenever I get stuck, despite his insistence that he's "a horrible teacher."

Contents

Preface

THE FIRST WEBSITE I ever designed from scratch was based on the website of a well-known luxury goods company. It was a complicated design, with lots of Flash-based accordians and sliders—quite a challenge for someone who knew only the most basic HTML and almost no CSS. Too impatient to learn what I needed to in Flash, I turned to JavaScript, rollover effects, and simple animated GIFs. I still cringe at the thought of it, even though it probably wasn't as bad as I remember.

Even though the user interface of that first design was almost identical to the inspiration site, I put my own twist on it with a different layout for the sliders and my own color scheme. I've never been one of those designers who can look at a design problem and come up with an idea for how to approach it out of thin air. I need to look at other designs and my surroundings to come up with ideas.

When I got started with design, there weren't as many sources of inspiration directed at designers as there are today (or if there were, I had yet to find them). So I taught myself how to look for inspiration in everything around me. I'd turn to magazine layouts if I needed a new approach to a website layout. I'd look for color schemes in photographs. I'd find UI ideas in electronics. I was constantly on the lookout for sources of ideas to incorporate into my designs. It became a bit of an obsession, and I used to have folders of images tucked away for later reference and inspiration.

WHAT'S INCLUDED IN THIS BOOK

In this book, I'll share with you how to find ideas from your surroundings. By the time you finish reading this book, you'll be able to look at virtually anything—from the soda bottle on your desk to the design of a website you like to the architecture in your hometown—and find design inspiration. Beyond that, you'll also have the basis for how to *apply* that inspiration to your actual work.

The first part of the book will give a basis for what goes into a good design, and is meant to get everyone on the same page. For more advanced designers, it might be a bit basic, but it's still a good idea to at least glance over it to make sure we're using the same terminology.

From there, I'll move on to cover both direct and indirect sources of ideas. Everything from websites to architecture to product packaging to photography is included. I break down how I look at some of the images included in each section, but each section has plenty of images without commentary so you can look over them and find your own ideas, without outside influence. It's an important skill you'll need to learn. No one is going to be there to tell you which ideas to use in the real world.

Finally, I've created two designs based on inspiration. The first is based on websites featured earlier in the book. The second is based on images of indirect idea sources, things like textures, photos, and artwork. I break down exactly how I use elements in each, to give you an idea of how you might incorporate your own inspiration.

There's a bonus chapter at the end that should give you a few more ideas for how to find inspiration, based on my own process.

I

FINDING
INSPIRATION

TYPES OF INSPIRATION

1

THERE ARE TWO basic kinds of inspiration available to web designers: direct inspiration, which consists of other website designs; and abstract inspiration, which consists of everything else. It's important for designers to learn to use both kinds of inspiration if they want to come up with original, unique designs.

Relying solely on inspiration from other website designs can be great for solving specific site-related problems, as you can see how others have handled the same issues in a real-world environment. But if everyone just studies designs that have already been done, innovation will be slow, or even nonexistent. Looking for inspiration outside the world of web design can present you with ideas that haven't been tried before, leading to faster innovation and better designs in the long run.

ABSTRACT INSPIRATION

Abstract inspiration is often harder to find and implement effectively than direct inspiration. When you see a website design, it's easy to draw inspiration from a header, a footer, or another part of the design. With abstract inspiration, you don't have such concrete elements to draw from. Instead, you need to learn to look at different aspects of an image, things like color and shape, texture and pattern.

COLOR

The color in an abstract source of inspiration is one of the easiest things to draw from. Colors are obvious; in many cases, they're the first thing we notice about an object or an image.

Taking a color scheme from a source of non-design inspiration is one of the simplest places to start. Look at the colors of an image or object and think about how they relate to one another. In some cases, a natural color scheme will emerge almost effortlessly, and in other cases, you'll need to do a bit more experimenting.

Figure 1-1: This photo has a very obvious color scheme of green, orange, and beige.
SOURCE: http://www.flickr.com/photos/smoorenburg/3503218892/ © Angie Garrett

Not all objects or images are suited to drawing a color scheme from. You want to look for things that have a variety of shades and tones, so that there's a range of colors to choose from. Good contrast is necessary in creating a color scheme that works for a design, not just one that's pretty to look at. Without sufficient contrast, the elements of a design blend together. When colors have good contrast, they stand out from one another, with some becoming more visually prominent than others. This helps reinforce the hierarchy of elements on the page.

Beyond drawing direct color schemes from an image, there's also using the colors present as a basis for the mood of your color scheme. You might just pull one color from an image and use that as the basis for creating a color scheme. For example, if there's a particularly striking shade of yellow in an image, you might use that as the starting point for a happy, upbeat design.

An image composed of mostly blues and grays might be used as the basis for the color scheme of a corporate design.

Figure 1-2: The photo here, while it has a good variety of colors, doesn't have a clearly defined color scheme.
Source: http://www.flickr.com/photos/emilyrides/4569081680/
© Michael Dolan

Figure 1-3: Pulling just one color from this and building a color scheme around it would work best.
Source: http://www.flickr.com/photos/qilin/4117559936/
© Christopher (Augapfel)

Figure 1-4: A subtle color scheme, but with good contrast.
Source: http://www.flickr.com/photos/calsidyrose/4131372530/
© Calsidyrose

SHAPE

Shape is almost as obvious as color in many cases. We can pick out organic, fluid shapes, or we can pick out geometric shapes like squares, triangles, and stars.

Figure 1-5: This image is filled with geometric shapes.
Source: http://www.flickr.com/photos/uggboy/4299149608/
©UggBoyUggGirl

Organic shapes can often be harder to incorporate into a design, as websites are often built around a basic structural grid. But they can still be used to create graphics or the general flow of content on a page.

Look at the shapes not only in the positive space of an image, but also in the negative space. The shapes created by a lack of content in an image or object can often be more striking, visually, than those in the object itself.

There's a difference in the feeling geometric and organic shapes give to the visitor. Geometric shapes usually add to a sense of structure and order on a page. They're formal and traditional. Organic shapes can give a more relaxed feeling to a design. They're unconventional and sometimes unexpected. Circles, because they're both fluid (with no angles or edges) and structured (a very regular, predictable shape), can be made to provide either feel to a design.

TEXTURES

Textures are subtler than outright shapes or colors. The type of texture present in an image or object is largely dependent on what the content is. In a photo of a tree, for example, the bark of the tree would be one texture, the leaves might be another, as might whatever is at the base of the tree, such as fallen leaves or dirt.

Textures are often organic in nature, and when found in the "real world" are often very tactile. It's uncommon for geometric shapes or other highly structured elements to be present in a true texture (they're more common in patterns).

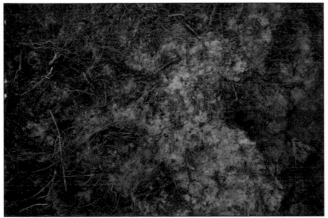

Textures are excellent to incorporate into the backgrounds or graphics of a website. Sometimes the addition of a texture can take a site from bland and predictable to polished and unique, without any other changes.

PATTERNS

Patterns are often composed of repeating geometry. They might be polka dots, brickwork (either real or simulated), or some other image. The main difference between a pattern and a texture, though, is that a pattern repeats.

Seamlessly repeating (or tiling) patterns are commonly used as backgrounds in website designs. They can add visual interest, contribute to the mood or tone of a site, and otherwise provide a more "finished" look to some designs. Of course, like any design element, patterns can contribute to a sense of visual clutter to your design when overused. It's a good idea to use them sparingly and subtly unless a loud aesthetic is what you're aiming for.

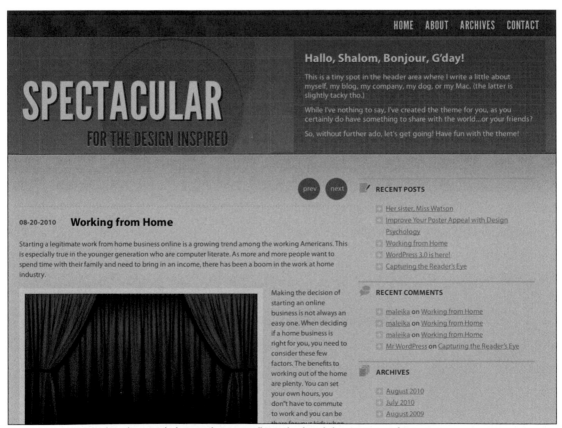

Figure 1-8: The Spectacular theme has a simple design made more visually complex through the extensive use of textures.
Source: http://www.smashingmagazine.com © Smashing Magazine / Maleika Esther Attawel

NEGATIVE SPACE

Some images are densely packed with content. There's little space where nothing is happening. The result is often vibrant, busy, and sometimes hectic. They give a definite mood and tone that is further influenced and defined by the other elements used. Oftentimes, the tone and mood in these designs is one of energy, vibrancy, and movement.

Figure 1-10: There's almost no negative space present in this image.

Other images have lots of empty space, where there aren't any overt visual elements. This negative space can often have just as dramatic an impact as an image that's largely occupied with "things." Look at the negative space (or lack thereof) in an image or object, and incorporate that into your design.

Figure 1-11: The negative space here is quite obvious, and fills up the majority of the image.
Source: http://www.flickr.com/photos/81659047@N00/5054907845/ © Elycia

WHERE TO FIND ABSTRACT INSPIRATION

Abstract inspiration is found all around us. Look around your desk, outside your office window, and virtually anywhere else, and you'll find abstract sources of inspiration. Start looking at these things as sources of inspiration, rather than just objects, and you'll likely start to find design ideas flowing into your head as you look around, without having to go looking for them.

DIRECT INSPIRATION

Direct inspiration is probably more familiar to most designers than abstract inspiration. Looking at another website as a source of design inspiration can be a great idea if you need help figuring out how to tackle a specific user interface problem. But if you're not careful, it can also result in a design that is too similar to the original. One of the worst things designers can do is to copy the design of another, especially if they try to pass it off as an original, which can easily happen when you don't understand why a design works and instead copy from it verbatim.

It's important to look critically at why a certain element in a design worked and what problem it solved. Without that understanding, it won't matter how adept you are at reusing elements from other designs. Your designs will almost always fail to live up to the success of the original.

When you're drawing inspiration from the work of someone else, it's imperative that you are very mindful of how much you're taking from the designer, and how close your design resembles the original. One of the best ways to avoid copying another site is to draw your inspiration from many sites, adapting elements of each and making them your own.

There are a ton of different elements you can draw inspiration from: headers, footers, sidebars, typography, color schemes, the general layout, color scheme, patterns or textures, and other graphical elements.

HEADERS, FOOTERS, AND SIDEBARS

Study the header, footer, and sidebar(s) of a site, and look at their relationships to one another. The size and shape of each of these elements is one thing you might be inspired by, as is the content and, in the case of sidebars, their position.

Headers are often either large, bold affairs, taking up a large portion of the screen when a page loads. There are plenty of examples of this kind of header out there.

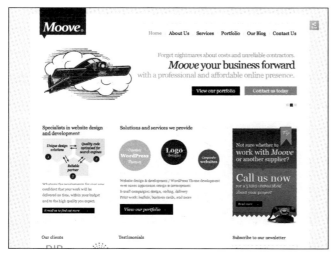

Figure 1-12: One example of a large header.
Source: http://www.mooveagency.com/ © Moove Agency LTD

Another common type of header is one that's small, often with just the site name and logo, and basic navigation or a search bar.

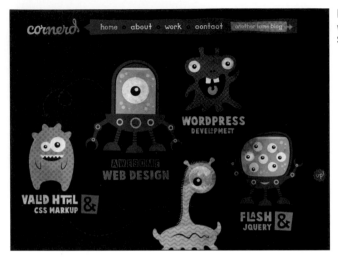

Figure 1-13: A great example of a smaller header, which takes up very little of the screen.
Source: http://www.cornerd.com/ © Cornerd

Sidebars may be on the left or right of a page (and sometimes even the center, though that's rare). Some sites use a single sidebar while others use multiples, and some sites use no sidebars at all.

Figure 1-14: A design with no sidebars, which creates a very streamlined style.
Source: http://thedangerbrain.com/ © The Danger Brain

Footers are often overlooked in website design. All too many sites just put basic copyright or other information in their footer, without including anything of use to the majority of site visitors. Look at how other sites have handled their footers to find ideas to make use of the space.

Figure 1-15: Footers are a great place to put extra information that doesn't fit elsewhere.
Source: http://jewellandginnie.com/ © Jewell & Ginnie

Figure 1-16: Footers can contain more than one kind of content.
Source: http://www.southernsavers.com/ © Southern Savers

Figure 1-17: Repeating a logo in the footer can reinforce a site's branding and add interest to a simple footer.

Source: http://theborsky.com/ © Shawn Borsky

GENERAL LAYOUT

The general layout of a site is another great place to draw inspiration. Is it a grid? Two columns? Three columns? Horizontal? What is the proportion of one element to another? What elements are included (or excluded)? How does the layout establish a hierarchy and visual flow? All of these are valid questions to ask when studying the layout of another site for inspiration.

If you use elements from the layout of another site, make sure that the other parts of the site are drastically different. Layout can be one of the easiest things to recognize from one site to another, and if you don't draw your other inspiration from other sources, it's likely someone will recognize the design.

Figure 1-18: A grid design with three columns.
Source: http://immersus.com/
© Immersus Media

Figure 1-19: Another grid design, with both three- and four-column sections.
Source: http://www.printmornyc.com/ © Print Mor NYC

Figure 1-20: A simple layout, with varying columns based on the content.
Source: http://www.sonic-iceland.com/ © Sonic Iceland

Figure 1-21: A grid-based layout with an emphasis on images.
Source: http://www.neveinspired.com/ © Neve Inspired

COLOR SCHEME

The color scheme of a site can be a great place to start. Again, though, this is a very recognizable part of some designs, and so you should use caution when incorporating inspiration like this.

Sometimes the best course of action when drawing inspiration from another site's color scheme is to pick only one or two colors, and then build your own color scheme around those. For the most part, you can reuse colors that appear in another design without worrying about infringing on another designer's intellectual property. There are exceptions to this, though, as some companies have trademarked particular colors.

Cadbury, for instance, has trademarked the color purple. The good news here is that the only time you can't use purple in a design is if the site you were designing was for a direct competitor to Cadbury (such as another chocolate or candy company). Even then, unless Cadbury can prove that the use of the color is likely to cause confusion among consumers, you would still likely be fine in using purple (so you might be able to get away with using purple as an accent color on a site that had a color palette made up of mostly other colors, but not as the primary color). Before deciding on a final color scheme, though, it's a good idea to find out whether there are any competing companies that may have trademarked a particular color.

Another way to draw inspiration from a color scheme is to simply copy the mood or tone of the colors, rather than the colors themselves. You might like the dark, brooding mood that a color scheme comprised of jewel tones gives, and might design a color scheme that gives the same impression, but uses different colors.

PATTERNS AND TEXTURES

The patterns and textures used in a site may or may not be publicly available for your own designs. If they are, or are licensed, there's nothing wrong with using exactly the same pattern or texture in your own design. In that case, though, you'll likely want to use it in a different way than the inspiring site. Just remember that very distinct patterns and textures may be recognized among sites, which makes your design appear less unique. You may want to create your own patterns and textures for anything more complex than a simple texture.

Figure 1-22: The Interlink Conference website uses grunge textures throughout their design.
Source: http://interlinkconference.com/ © Interlink Conference

Figure 1-23: The Atlas website uses grunge textures in their background only.
Source: http://iheartatlas.com/portfolio.html © Atlas

If the pattern or texture is proprietary, you can use something that evokes a similar mood. A lot of sites out there, for example, use paper textures. There are thousands of paper textures out there that are available for free or low cost, and it's easy to create your own, too. Consider using a texture that's similar but recognizably different from the source design. Rather than using something like a grid-paper texture, you might use one that's lined or dotted. Or instead of using a mossy, rocky texture, you might use a stained concrete texture that has a similar color scheme.

Figure 1-24: Backseat Vintage uses a dark wood grain images as their background.
Source: http://backseatvintage.bigcartel.com/ © Backseat Vintage

Figure 1-25: Firefly Tonics also uses a wood grain background image.
Source: http://www.fireflytonics.com/ © Firefly Tonics

TYPOGRAPHY

Typography is probably one of the richest areas to draw inspiration from. Everything from line height to the typefaces used can lend inspiration to your design. Using developer tools like Firebug makes it simple to see the CSS and HTML that are used for creating specific typographical designs.

Regardless of what kind of typography inspiration you're looking for, make sure that the design you're drawing from has well-thought-out typography that adheres to basic typographical principles. When looking for ideas for something like body copy, for example, look for other designs that have exceptionally readable text.

Look at the font choices (including the type of font), sizes, line heights, type colors (and background color), and styles applied to things like links or headers. It's also a good idea to see how the typography interacts with other elements on the page, how much space is around it, and how it balances with imagery. Is the type meant to be as elegantly quiet as possible (see Figure 1-26) so the content shines through without distraction, or is it meant to be illustrative (see Figure 1-27)?

With the increase in web fonts use, there are literally thousands of possible typographical designs out there that you can choose from, or use as inspiration to create your own.

Figure 1-26: Thought Catalog often has long articles, and readability is key.
Source: http://thoughtcatalog.com/ © Thought Catalog

Figure 1-27: The Frank's website has varied, well-designed typography.
Source: http://hotdogscoldbeer.com/ © Frank's Hot Dogs • Cold Beer

OTHER GRAPHICAL ELEMENTS

Other graphics within a design can also be used as the basis for creating your own project's graphical styles. Within an e-commerce design, for example, how many images are included for each product? Are they displayed as thumbnails? Full-size images? In a slideshow or other animation? On a blog you might look at whether images are used for each post, and how they're formatted (centered, on the left or right with text wrapping around them, and so on.).

Look at the way graphics are used on a site, and whether they're there to improve usability, contribute to content, or serve some other function.

DON'T COPY

The line between being inspired by something and copying it is often thin. Website designs are considered intellectual property, and are covered by copyright laws in most countries. That includes both the front-end design and the code that it was created with.

One way to avoid copying another site is to draw your inspiration from as many sources as possible, including more abstract sources. Take your color scheme from a photograph, your general layout from a magazine article, your background texture from a site you like, and your typography from a different site. In this way, you're not copying any particular design, and the design you come up with won't resemble any of the sources closely enough to be recognizable.

WHAT MAKES A GOOD DESIGN? 2

THERE ARE HUNDREDS of millions of websites out there, and obviously they're not all well designed. Even some of the more popular sites on the Internet have designs that one wouldn't necessarily consider "good."

So what makes a design "good" or "bad"? Are there hard-and-fast rules that a designer should follow when designing, or is it more open to interpretation?

The answer is yes. There are rules for good design that designers should at least consider, but good design is also open to interpretation. Sometimes going against the rules can result in a site that's better than anything that could have been achieved abiding by all the "rules." But before you start breaking rules, you first need to know what they are.

VISUAL BALANCE

Visual balance generally refers to whether a design is symmetrical or asymmetrical (and whether that asymmetry is jarring or works within the design). Some designs are based entirely around a perfectly symmetrical layout. Symmetrical designs are generally more straightforward to create than asymmetrical designs.

Figure 2-1: A symmetrical design.
Source: http://www.forefathersgroup.com © Forefathers Group

In an asymmetrical design, balance is still important. One side of the design can't overwhelm the other side. But, as a general rule, asymmetrical designs are more visually interesting than symmetrical designs as they're less predictable and often cause more movement of the eye, so the added difficulty in properly balancing them is sometimes worth it.

Most website designs are asymmetrical, with the exception of some three-column sites with sidebars on each side, and some single-column sites. But even in a symmetrical design, the arrangement of content can create a more asymmetrical feel (such as placing images aligned to the right or left of a blog post). When designing either a symmetrical or asymmetrical design, make sure you take into account how the content will affect the visual balance of the end design.

Figure 2-2: An asymmetrical design.
Source: http://esbeuno.noahstokes.com © Noah Stokes

COLOR

The color scheme of a website can make or break the design. Color is the most tangible part of good design, and the easiest thing to emulate. Although visual balance often has a subtle psychological effect on a site's visitors, it can be hard for people to put their fingers on exactly why it's affecting them. Color, on the other hand, has a much more pronounced effect, and can often be identified as the root source of an impression without too much exploration.

Shades of a color are created by adding black to the original hue. Tints are created by adding white to the original hue. Tones are created by adding gray to the original hue.

Colors can have different meanings in different cultures, so be sure to check the meaning of a particular hue in the culture of a site's target market before using it. For example, white is often associated with innocence and purity in the West, but is associated with death in other cultures.

A successful color scheme for a design needs more than just a set of coordinating colors. It also needs colors with sufficient contrast. Colors that all have similar intensities don't work well together. Instead, you need colors of varying intensities. Black and white are the most obvious contrasting colors, but combining shades, tints, and tones of various colors works well, too.

TRADITIONAL COLOR SCHEMES

There are seven basic color scheme patterns: monochromatic, analogous, complementary, split complementary, triadic, tetradic, and square. Understanding these different color scheme patterns is helpful not only for creating your own website designs, but also for evaluating the designs of others.

Monochromatic color schemes are made up of different shades, tints, or tones of a single color. For example, a navy blue, royal blue, and light blue color scheme is monochromatic.

Figure 2-3: A monochromatic color scheme.

An analogous color scheme is made up of three colors that are next to each other on the twelve-part color wheel. Red-orange, red, and red-violet are an example of an analogous color scheme.

Figure 2-4: An analogous color scheme.

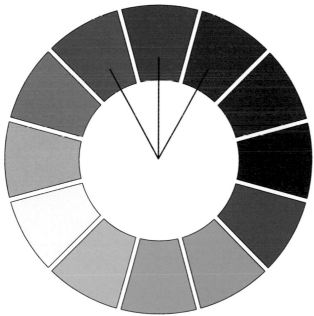

Complementary color schemes are made up of colors opposite each other on the twelve-part color wheel. Green and red, blue and orange, and purple and yellow are all examples of complementary color schemes. Be wary of designs using these; when used in their pure forms next to each other, they simulate actual movement and vibration along the border, which is uncomfortable to look at.

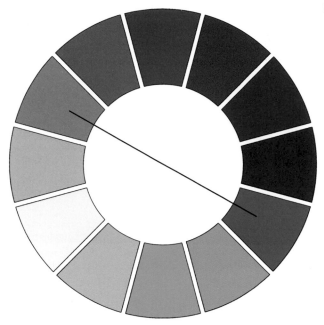

Figure 2-5: A complementary color scheme.

Split complementary color schemes are made up of the colors on either side of a single color's complement. For example, a color scheme of green, red-orange, and red-violet is split complementary.

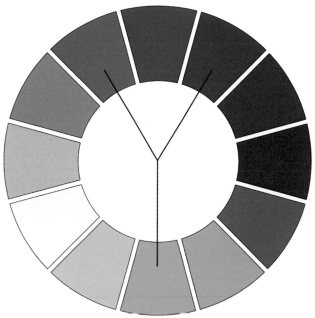

Figure 2-6: A split complementary color scheme.

Tetradic color schemes could be thought of as split-split complementary. In other words, they're made up of colors on either side of two complementary colors. You can also think of them as a pair of complementary color schemes, one step apart on the twelve-part color wheel. Red-orange, red-violet, yellow-green, and blue-green make up a tetradic color scheme.

Figure 2-7: A tetradic color scheme.

A square color scheme is made up of four colors that are equidistant on the twelve-part color wheel (two complementary color schemes, two steps apart on the wheel). Blue, orange, yellow-green, and red-violet make up an example of a square color scheme.

Figure 2-8: A square color scheme.

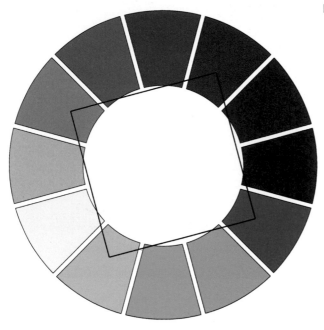

Most designs don't follow traditional color schemes to the letter, and instead incorporate different tones, tints, and shades of colors included in a scheme for better contrast and visual interest. Colors are rarely used in the same proportion, with some colors being used as accents, others for the background, and others for different design elements. The combination of using different tones, tints, and shades, along with different amounts of each color, is what creates a visually interesting and successful design.

PROPORTION

The relative size of things within a design is referred to as *proportion*. The proportion of things on a site has a direct effect on their priority. Visually, larger objects are more likely to gain attention over smaller objects, all other things being equal.

Figure 2-9: An example of proportion in practice. Varying the size of the grid squares creates visual interest. Source: http://www.codaautomotive.com/ © CODA Automotive, Inc.

In design, this means that as a general rule, more important elements should be larger than less important elements. Good designs use proportion to draw the eye to certain elements of the design or content, whereas poor designs generally miss this important factor.

PRIORITY

There's always a priority within a design, but how that priority is represented visually varies widely. When visitors to your website view a page, the most important parts of that page should immediately catch their eyes. If it doesn't, then the page can come across as having no real purpose.

Figure 2-10: An example of priority in practice. Notice how the bright colors, combined with white space, draw attention to particular parts of the site. Source: http://www.styleandconscience.com © Montreal Couture

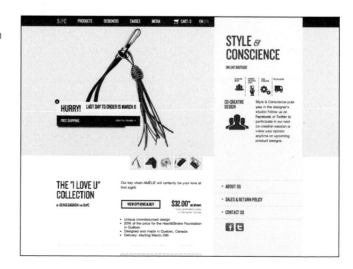

The priority of an element can be affected by multiple factors. Color plays a huge factor. A color that contrasts with the rest of a design will call attention to itself (which is why you often see call-to-action buttons in a color that contrasts with the rest of a site's design, so it stands out more). Proportion is also a big factor, with larger items appearing to have a higher priority than smaller items.

RHYTHM

There are a few different kinds of rhythm commonly used in design: progressive, regular, and flowing. All three have a direct effect on how people interact with a design, by directing their eyes through the content on a page.

Progressive rhythm is a sequence of elements, progressing from one to the next. Sometimes, elements overlap. In other cases, the progression might be in size (such as smaller to larger) or color (such as lighter to darker). Progressive rhythms often show a direct relationship between elements.

Regular rhythms show elements repeating in a regular interval or pattern. Grid-based designs often have a very regular rhythm. This kind of rhythm is often very formal and organized.

Flowing rhythms are more organic, with no defined pattern. Think of flowing water in a stream: it's all going in roughly the same direction, but it's not all moving in an identical fashion. Flowing rhythms are harder to achieve, but are sometimes more striking visually.

The purpose of any rhythm is to direct the visitor in a pattern that the designer has devised. Rhythm gives a sense of order to a design, and can help ground the visitor.

Figure 2-11: Progressive rhythm.
Source: http://www.flickr.com/photos/charlotte
morrall/3587039559/ © Charlotte Morrall

Figure 2-12: Regular rhythm.
Source: http://www.flickr.com/photos/vinoth
chandar/4257167174/ © Vinoth Chandar

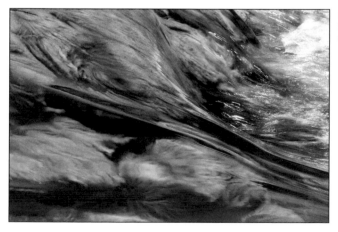

Figure 2-13: Flowing rhythm.
Source: http://www.flickr.com/photos/iandeth/2485322567/
© Toshimasa Ishibashi

UNITY

Any good design needs to be unified. Every element has to work with every other element, or the result is jarring. Without unity, a design can appear haphazard and accidental, and can be hard for a visitor to navigate.

There are a number of ways to unify a design, but the most common way is through repetition. Elements within the design, such as textures, patterns, colors, and graphical styles, should be repeated throughout a design, to ground the visitor. Every element should work harmoniously, to present a consistent image.

Figure 2-14: Repeating colors and textures throughout create a nicely unified design.
Source: http://www.rueverte.com/ © Rue Verte

PURPOSE

This chapter has discussed all the visual elements of a great design, but there's one other very important principle that you need to take into account when you're looking for inspiration: the purpose of the design and of its elements.

Without a clear purpose, a design can become aimless. Each element within the design needs to serve and support a central purpose. This purpose is going to vary depending on the particular site. It's tied closely to the mood and style of a site, which are very important in how well a site serves its purpose.

The purpose is also tied closely to problem solving within a design. Rather than just looking at the elements in a design, it's important to look at why those elements were used. Why did the designer choose navy blue and gray as the color scheme for an accounting firm's site? (The answer probably has to do with the fact that navy is a very sturdy, loyal color, whereas gray is associated with responsibility and stability.) Why did another designer choose to use a visible grid layout for a magazine site? (Probably because it's easier to organize large amounts of content within a grid.)

Think about the different ways great designers solve the problems presented to them by the requirements of a site, and try to figure out why they chose one solution over another. To further test and improve your own skills, see if you can come up with a better solution to the same problem. But take the time to understand why the designer chose the original solution.

HOW TO LOOK AT DESIGNS

When most people look at a design, they don't bother to quantify why it does or doesn't work. But as a designer, it's important to dissect why a particular design works or doesn't work. To do that, you'll need to break down the different parts of the design.

Look at the way the design follows or breaks the rules covered in this chapter. Some designs will work in spite of breaking a rule or two, but most more or less follow them.

To get an idea of how some of the elements of a site work together, it can be helpful to break the site down into a wireframe. This is useful for looking at things like proportion, rhythm, and priority, although obviously it does little for color scheme or unity, and is limited in viewing visual balance.

Figure 2-15: An example wireframe.

Figure out if the color scheme follows any of the traditional color schemes, or if it breaks free from them. Don't forget to look at tones, tints, and shades of the colors within a design, as those aspects can give more insight into how the color scheme was created.

Look to see if any elements stand out from the rest, or if they clash. This indicates issues with unity in the design, although sometimes there's a purpose behind a clashing element (such as making a call-to-action stand out).

Practice will teach you how to better dissect a design, and will make it easier for you to use particular elements to inspire your own work within a design without copying.

INSPIRING
IMAGES

WEBSITE DESIGNS

3

DRAWING INSPIRATION FROM the website designs of others is probably one of the easiest places to start. But with the hundreds of millions of websites out there, it can quickly get overwhelming when trying to find specific examples of certain kinds of sites.

There are three basic ways to look for inspiring websites. You can look by style (such as grunge, minimalist, or colorful). You can look by type (blog, portfolio, e-commerce, and so on). Or you can look by industry (like hospitality, fashion, or technology).

If you or your client already has an idea of how you want the site to look, searching for sites by style makes the most sense. If you're unsure of the look and feel of the site, try looking by the type of site or by the industry of the company for ideas. Checking out other sites in the same industry can be particularly useful in figuring out what kinds of content are usually included on a site, as well as what visitors are likely to expect and what the industry norms are.

DRAWING INSPIRATION FROM WEBSITE STYLES

There are dozens of website styles out there, and they fall in and out of favor on a regular basis. But there are a handful of broad styles that seem to stay pretty consistently popular, regardless of current trends—minimal and clean sites; grunge and retro sites; bright and colorful sites; and organic and handmade-style sites.

Each style can be adapted to fit a wide variety of sites. There's often some overlap, too, with sites that fit into both the minimal and grunge, or organic and retro categories, for just two examples.

Be careful mixing too many styles, though, as that can just lead to a haphazard design. It's important to have clear goals in mind before you start designing. Mixing unexpected elements can greatly improve your designs, but limit this to one or two elements for the best results.

MINIMAL AND CLEAN

It was Leonardo da Vinci who said, "Simplicity is the ultimate sophistication." Minimalist and clean websites echo this very sentiment. They include nothing in their designs that is not absolutely vital to the site and its ability to do what it was designed to do.

Although clean and minimalist designs have been around in the web design world for a very long time, they have been enjoying a recent resurgence in popularity. Some might attribute this to current events, and the desire many people have to get some simplicity back into their lives. Whether that is the case or not, the web is a much more sophisticated place because of sites like those featured here.

Take the Brave Nu Digital site (Figure 3-1), for example. A simple white background behind the content combined with a basic grid layout creates a site that's unassuming and easy to look at. The addition of a patterned background on the sides of the site adds some visual interest without adding clutter. The entire thing feels very confident and understated, while communicating very clearly, exactly like a good minimalist design should.

The Sumit Paul site (Figure 3-2), on the other hand, has a bolder look. The dark blue, gray, and orange color scheme adds a lot of visual interest, but there's plenty of negative space to prevent things from looking cluttered or too busy, while ensuring the eye is guided to the most important elements. Using color bands to block out different sections of content also adds some organization to the site without being imposing.

With the sites included here, pay close attention to the balance of negative space, as well as to the way emphasis is placed on one element or another within the designs. This is often where the strength of a great minimalist or clean website design is most apparent.

Figure 3-1
Source: http://bravenudigital.com © Brave Nu Digital

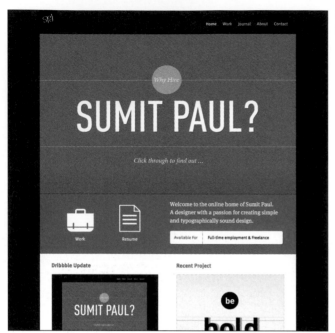

Figure 3-2
Source: http://www.sumitpaul.com © Sumit Paul

Figure 3-3
Source: http://www.bendarby.co.uk © Ben Darby

Figure 3-4
Source: http://fusionads.net © Bold

Figure 3-5
Source: http://eighthourday.com © Eight Hour Day

Figure 3-6
Source: http://www.fortherecord.simonfosterdesign.com/
© Simon Foster

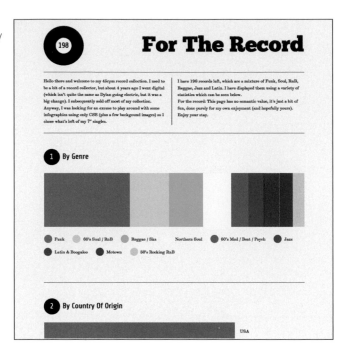

Figure 3-7
Source: http://www.thesum.ca © TH= SUM

Figure 3-8
Source: http://www.nicelyreplayed.com © re:play Creative

Figure 3-9
Source: http://www.gesturetheory.com © Gesture Theory

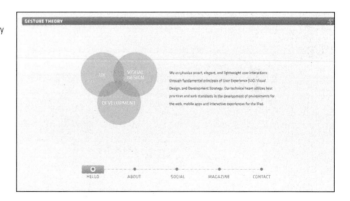

Figure 3-10
Source: http://heckhouse.com © Bethany Heck

Figure 3-11
Source: http://nordkapp.fi © Nordkapp

Figure 3-12
Source: http://www.elegantseagulls.com © Elegant Seagulls

Figure 3-13
Source: http://bygonebureau.com © Bygone Bureau

Figure 3-14
Source: http://williamflagello.com © William Flagello

Figure 3-15
Source: http://damianherrington.co.uk © Damian Herrington

Figure 3-16
Source: http://www.gradeonedigital.com © Gradeone Digital

Figure 3-17
Source: http://hatbox.co © HatBox

Figure 3-18
Source: http://juliaparris.com © Julia Parris. Designed by Able Parris, developed by Brett Buddin

Figure 3-19
Source: http://work.mabu.dk © Mads Burcharth

Figure 3-20
Source: http://www.bangbangphoto.co.uk © Bang Bang Photo

GRUNGE AND RETRO

Grunge and retro designs once belonged almost purely on personal websites. It was rare to see them on corporate sites or even as portfolio sites. All that has changed in the past few years, as more and more companies embrace grunge and retro styling.

Most grunge designs look just a little bit worn, like your favorite pair of jeans or an old T-shirt. Paper and other textures are common, as are torn and taped effects. Grunge designs look a little bit (or sometimes a lot) dirty, like they've seen better days. A little bit of grunge can be perfectly appropriate on almost any kind of site, even corporate sites.

Retro and vintage-style designs sometimes incorporate grunge elements, but not always. Some retro designs are clean and polished. The main thing retro sites have in common is that they'd look right at home a few decades (or a century or two) ago.

The Amazee Labs site (Figure 3-21) has a strong retro vibe, with just a little bit of grunge. The textured background is a popular grunge motif, as are the slightly worn graphics. But the simple color scheme and friendly typography give the site a squarely retro feeling, too.

The Word Refuge site (Figure 3-22) has a much more antique style to it, while still retaining some grunge elements. The textured background is grungy, while the other graphics are all retro. The light use of bright red accents adds visual interest and value through its scarcity, and steps the design up a notch.

Stephen Caver's site (Figure 3-23) has a very subtle grunge feel to it, and the color scheme makes it feel a little bit retro. The background is slightly textured and distressed looking, but is offset by the bold typography in the header. It's a great example of combining grunge with minimalism.

Look to how grunge and retro elements are used in ways that aren't expected in the images in this section, as well as the common elements most of the sites share (like worn textures). Also look at how the grunge or vintage elements reinforce the message or purpose of the designs.

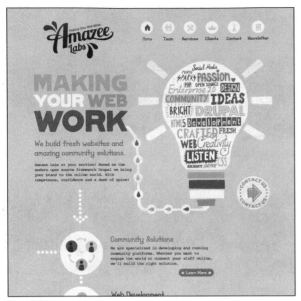

Figure 3-21
Source: http://www.amazeelabs.com © Amazee Labs

Figure 3-23
Source: http://www.stephencaver.com © Stephen Caver

Figure 3-22
Source: http://www.wordrefuge.com © Word Refuge

Figure 3-24
Source: http://popchartlab.com © Pop Chart Lab

Figure 3-25
Source: http://molecube.ca © Molecube

Figure 3-27
Source: http://www.gagesalzano.com © Gage Salzano

Figure 3-26
Source: http://webislove.com © Michela Chiucini

Figure 3-28
Source: http://www.cascadebreweryco.com.au © Cascade Brewery Co

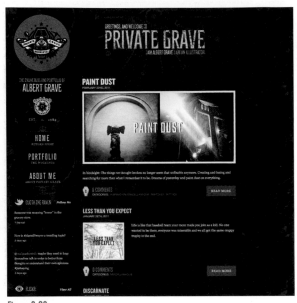

Figure 3-29
Source: http://www.privategrave.com © Albert Grave

Figure 3-31
Source: http://www.designnus.cl © Felipe Medina

Figure 3-30
Source: http://kennysaunders.com © Kenny Saunders

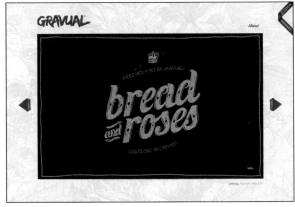

Figure 3-32
Source: http://www.gravual.com © Gravual

Figure 3-33
Source: http://www.goldenboymedia.co.uk © Goldenboy Media

Figure 3-35
Source: http://www.city-dog.co.uk © City Dog. Designed by Impero Design

Figure 3-34
Source: http://www.mobeldesign.nu © Mobeldesign

Figure 3-36
Source: http://foreverheavy.com © Forever Heavy

Figure 3-37
Source: http://fieldnotesbrand.com © Field Notes

Figure 3-39
Source: http://www.brooklynslate.com © Brooklyn Slate Company

Figure 3-38
Source: http://thesearethings.com © These Are Things

Figure 3-40
Source: http://visualrepublic.net © Visual Republic

BRIGHT AND COLORFUL

Bright and colorful designs are seen across virtually every kind of site online. There are a couple of ways to approach this kind of design, with varying levels of difficulty. First, you can create a site that has a fairly neutral color scheme, with one or two bright pops of color. Alternatively, you can use a bright but basically monochromatic color scheme. Finally, you can combine a number of bright colors, although it's difficult to do this without overwhelming your content.

The HTML5Lab site (Figure 3-41) takes the first approach to using color. The light blue background is broken up nicely with bright patches of red. It leaves the site with a lively feeling, without being overpowering.

Color theory is particularly important when it comes to designing bright and colorful sites. Make sure you familiarize yourself with the meanings of different colors in the culture of the site's target market to avoid sending the wrong message.

Netlife Research (Figure 3-49) uses a very bright shade of apple green for the bulk of its site, with white and black accents. It's very strong visually, but also has a nice sense of uniformity and order.

Heath Waller is much bolder with the color choices for his website (Figure 3-53). He uses a color scheme of bright cyan and red, with a photo background that also brings in magenta and orange. It's a bold choice, for sure, but works well here and creates a design that's unlikely to be forgotten.

Obviously, the colors used in the designs included here are a great source of ideas. But look at how the colors are used, the message and mood they deliver, and the balance of one color to another. Remember, too, that color can have an intensely personal effect on the viewer. Consider how the colors in each design here make you feel, and then compare that to the traditional color meanings for further evidence of the power of color.

Figure 3-41
Source: http://html5lab.pl © Dab Hand Studio

Figure 3-43
Source: http://www.imfrom.me © IMFROM.ME

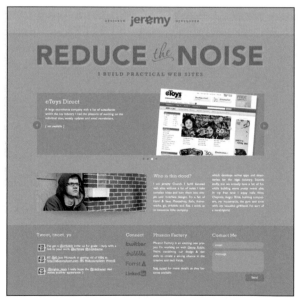

Figure 3-42
Source: http://j.eremy.net © Jeremy Church

Figure 3-44
Source: http://www.jtown.org © Rasteroids Design

Figure 3-45
Source: http://www.clickmedia.pl © Click Media

Figure 3-47
Source: http://raycheung.me © Ray Cheung

Figure 3-46
Source: http://licornpublishing.com/accueil.php © Licorn Publishing

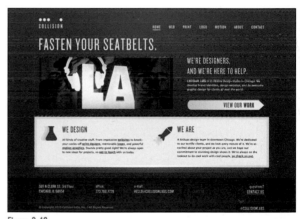

Figure 3-48
Source: http://collisionlabs.com © Collision Labs

Figure 3-49
Source: http://netliferesearch.com © Netlife Research

Figure 3-51
Source: http://inserviowebsolutions.co.uk © Inservio Web Solutions

Figure 3-50
Source: http://www.amoderneden.com © A Modern Eden

Figure 3-52
Source: http://www.icelab.com.au © Icelab Pty Ltd

Figure 3-53

Source: http://www.heathwaller.com © Heath Waller

Figure 3-55

Source: http://designdisease.com © Design Disease

Figure 3-54

Source: http://www.w3.org/html/logo © W3C

Figure 3-56

Source: http://smorge.com © Smorge

Figure 3-57

Source: http://coexhibitions.com © Co Exhibitions. Designed and developed by Permanent Art and Design Group

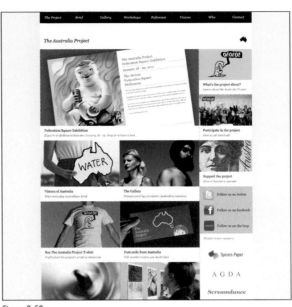

Figure 3-59

Source: http://www.australiaproject.com © The Australia Project

Figure 3-58

Source: http://www.jaradjohnson.com © Jarad Johnson Design

Figure 3-60

Source: http://www.manchestercraftmafia.co.uk © Manchester Craft Mafia

ORGANIC AND HANDMADE

Organic and handmade sites aren't as common as the other styles included here, but they are growing more popular, especially among certain demographics and types of sites. Part of this might be attributable to the popularity of organic and natural products in our everyday lives, and our desire for the web to follow suit.

Organic and handmade style incorporates a lot of site design possibilities. The main thing they have in common is a more natural feeling than any of the other styles here. Hand-drawn elements are common, as are fluid shapes and color schemes derived from nature. They often have a softer look than many sites, and may incorporate retro and grunge elements.

The Happy Time Cafe's website (Figure 3-61) incorporates some hand-drawn elements into its collage-style header, as well as fluid shapes surrounding the content area. Keeping the main content area of the site in a more minimalist style keeps the design looking very professional, while still maintaining the organic feeling.

The True Tea site (Figure 3-67) uses a hand-drawn background and some subtle, natural textures. Coloring in the background image for the main content area is a nice touch that makes the design look more thoughtful. As is often the case with these kinds of sites, contrast is used very well–this time between the roughness of the illustration in the background and the sharpness of the bottle.

The random hand-drawn borders around the images on the Frocktastic site (Figure 3-69) add a lot of visual interest to a site that is otherwise black and white. Simple details like this can take a would-be generic design and turn it into something special.

The natural and organic elements in the sites here are most often found in designs for companies or topics closely related to nature or the organic industry. But consider designs that aren't directly related to these obvious types of sites, and how they might benefit from some of the design choices made in the designs included in this section.

Figure 3-61
Source: http://www.thehappytimecafe.com © The Happy Time
Cafe

Figure 3-62
Source: http://www.kathryncorneli.us © Kathryn Cornelius

Figure 3-63
Source: http://www.ipolecat.com/#home © Polecat

Figure 3-64
Source: http://www.andrinaperic.com © Andrina Peric
Photography

Figure 3-65
Source: http://www.made-in-england.com © Made in England

Figure 3-66
Source: http://www.phase2technology.com/design/
© Phase2Technology

Figure 3-67
Source: http://www.truetea.cz.en © True Tea

Figure 3-68

Source: http://www.lega-lega.com © MIT dizajn studio

Figure 3-69

Source: http://frocktastic.com © Frocktastic

Figure 3-70
Source: http://www.frankpr.it © Frank PR

Figure 3-71
Source: http://creaturetales.com.au © Creature Tales.
Designed by Studio Racket

Figure 3-72
Source: http://www.clairecolesdesign.co.uk © Claire Coles
Design. Designed by With Associates

Figure 3-73
Source: http://creativespaces.net.au © Creative Spaces: City of
Melbourne and Arts Victoria

Figure 3-74
Source: http://stillpointesanctuary.org © Still Pointe Llama
Sanctuary

Figure 3-75
Source: http://www.augustempress.com © August Empress

Figure 3-76
Source: http://kylesteed.com © Kyle Steed

Figure 3-77
Source: http://dropr.com © Dropr

Figure 3-78
Source: http://www.hellosoursally.com © Sour Sally

Figure 3-79
Source: http://www.deniseandrade.com © Boho Girl

Figure 3-80
Source: http://www.goinghometoroost.com © Going Home to Roost

DRAWING INSPIRATION BY WEBSITE TYPE

Different types of websites have different needs and design conventions. What looks great on a corporate site doesn't necessarily look so good on a portfolio. What works great on an e-commerce site might be awful on a personal website.

Studying different kinds of websites to see what works and what doesn't, depending on the specific purpose of the site, is a great way to get new ideas for your own projects. Don't be afraid to look at how other types of sites handle certain user interface challenges. Just because it hasn't been done on a certain type of site before doesn't mean it won't work.

BLOGS AND MAGAZINE SITES

Blogs and magazine sites, by their very nature, are heavy on text-based content. Typography, and especially readability, is vital to the success of these kinds of sites, as is good organization of content. Without those elements, a blog or magazine site is doomed to failure.

Of the three basic kinds of blogs (personal, topical, and corporate), there's a lot of variation in what works and what doesn't in terms of design. Personal blogs often reflect the content as well as the personality of their owner. Corporate blogs often mimic the design of the regular corporate website. The design of a topical blog should reflect the content. Magazine sites, on the other hand, often more closely mimic the design of their print counterpart (if there is one).

Laura Burciaga's blog (Figure 3-82) has a very elegant and polished look. Since she mostly discusses interior design and decorating, it makes sense for her blog to look the way it does. The site also has outstanding typography, managing to combine two serifs and a script typeface without any conflict.

IconEden's blog (Figure 3-84) is a great example of a corporate blog that isn't just a copy of their corporate site. Other than carrying over the wood-grain texture from their main site, their blog design is entirely unique, and so much better for it!

The blog of design company Tinder and Sparks (Figure 3-95) is a great adaptation of the rest of their website. What really sets it apart is the change they've made to their logo: on the portfolio section of their website, the company name is surrounded by rainbow-colored dots; on the blog, it's surrounded by rainbow-colored symbols (including a dragonfly, pig, and scissors).

When studying the designs in this section, pay close attention to how content, often largely text-based, is incorporated into the design. Blogs and magazine sites often have much more in-depth content-management needs than sites with more simplified content, and ideas gleaned from these sites can be invaluable when creating designs for any content-heavy site.

Figure 3-81

Source: http://retinart.net © Retinart

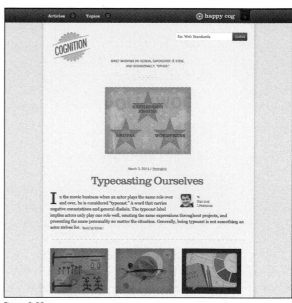

Figure 3-83

Source: http://cognition.happycog.com © Happy Cog

Figure 3-82

Source: http://lauraburciaga.com © Laura Burciaga. Designed by Ismael Burciaga

Figure 3-84

Source: http://www.iconeden.com/blog/ © IconEden.com & Frexy.com

Figure 3-85
Source: http://www.grainandgram.com © Grain & Gram

Figure 3-87
Source: http://trentwalton.com © Trent Walton

Figure 3-86
Source: http://hicksdesign.co.uk/journal/ © Hicksdesign

Figure 3-88
Source: http://bbqwar.com © Ismael Burciaga & BBQ War

Figure 3-89
Source: http://www.idsgn.org © IDSGN

Figure 3-91
Source: http://thepioneerwoman.com © The Pioneer Woman | Ree Drummond

Figure 3-90
Source: http://backpagefootball.com © Back Page Football

Figure 3-92
Source: http://thedarlingstarling.com © Elizabeth Shiver

Figure 3-93
Source: http://tomatotalk.earthfare.com © Earth Fare

Figure 3-95
Source: http://www.featureme.co.uk © Feature Me, design based on Sight theme by WPShower

Figure 3-94
Source: http://tinderandsparks.com/blog © Tinder and Sparks

Figure 3-96
Source: http://www.narfstuff.co.uk © Narfstuff

Figure 3-97
Source: http://www.flintandtinder.co.uk/tinderbox © Flint and Tinder

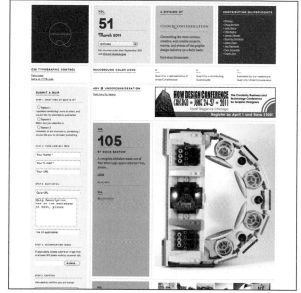

Figure 3-99
Source: http://www.underconsideration.com/quipsologies/ © UnderConsideration

Figure 3-98
Source: http://lanecrawford.com © Lane Crawford

E-COMMERCE SITES

The main purpose of an e-commerce site is to sell something. Sometimes it focuses on a single product, other times it's an entire catalog. In either case, an e-commerce site needs to consistently move visitors through a predetermined sales funnel.

Because of the wide variety of products for sale over the Internet, there's a huge amount of variation between different e-commerce sites. Virtually every style of site is seen, from black and white minimalist to grungy collages.

The Ashes and Milk website (Figure 3-101) uses a photo background, with content cleverly placed in various wooden boxes. It gives it a very unique look, and maintains a sense of minimalism. The photo-realism continues into their product listings, which appear to be an arrangement of printed photos. The entire site is very well thought out, with careful attention paid to even the smallest details.

Uppercase (Figure 3-102) has created a fantastically minimal site with just enough detail to make it really interesting. The whole thing feels clean and modern, but with a hint of classicism achieved through the inviting muted blue and white color scheme. The well-organized product listings are a dream for browsing.

Bohemia (Figure 3-105) uses a much more "traditional" e-commerce layout, with product categories listed across the top, a featured special/product slider, and more featured items below. But it's put together in such a seamless fashion that it deserves recognition. The use of subtle patterns and gradients, along with the careful attention paid to details that affect user experience, make it a hit where so many comparable sites are misses.

In addition to the visual design choices in made on the sites included here, pay attention to how they've approached the sales portion of the site design. Without a strong sales message, an e-commerce design is largely pointless.

Figure 3-100
Source: http://www.bonjourmoncoussin.com/en/ © Bonjour
Mon Coussin

Figure 3-101
Source: http://www.ashesandmilk.com © Ashes and Milk

Figure 3-102
Source: http://shop.uppercasegallery.ca © UPPERCASE publishing inc.

Figure 3-103
Source: http://www.narwhalcompany.com © Narwhal Co.
Design by Stephen Chai

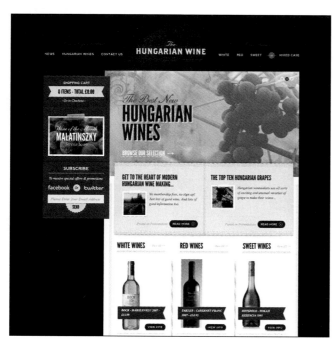

Figure 3-104
Source: http://www.hungarianwindesociety.co.uk © Hungarian Wines Society

Figure 3-105
Source: http://www.bohemiadesign.co.uk © Bohemia Design Ltd.

Figure 3-108
Source: http://hobancards.com © Hoban Press

Figure 3-109
Source: http://www.mariecatribs.com/store/ © Marie Catrib's

Figure 3-110
Source: http://www.makr.com © Makr Carry Goods

Figure 3-111
Source: http://www.exclusivereels.com/reels/f-series-collection
© Exclusive Reels, Ltd.

Figure 3-112
Source: http://oakstreetbootmakers.com © Oak Street
Bootmakers

Figure 3-113
Source: http://www.rfrmjewelry.com/necklaces/n031.php
© RFRM Jewelry. Designed by Knoed Creative

Figure 3-114
Source: http://www.kowtowclothing.com © Kowtow Clothing

Figure 3-115
Source: http://www.saturdaysnyc.com © Saturdays NYC

Figure 3-116
Source: http://www.dba-co.com/pen © DBA

Figure 3-117
Source: http://www.rfrmjewelry.com/necklaces/n031.php
© hard graft

Figure 3-118

Source: http://www.unitedpixelworkers.com © Full Stop
Interactive

COMPANY AND CORPORATE SITES

Corporate sites used to all look the same: they had color schemes that consisted of navy blue, burgundy, or hunter green, mixed with black and white. More progressive companies might have incorporated some gray. They had traditional layouts (two or three columns, with a header large enough for their logo and tag line), and usually all had the same generic stock photos. Trying to get corporate clients to do something different was near impossible.

Luckily, that's not the case anymore. Corporate clients, from law firms to real estate agencies to industrial manufacturers, are creating websites that are much more than a digital version of their paper brochures. There are now thousands of examples of great corporate websites out there, sometimes coming from very unlikely companies.

Take the Hunter's Wine website (Figure 3-119), for example. It has a clean, grid-based layout with a decidedly modern look (something that used to be quite rare for a company as traditional as a wine producer). The organization of content is impeccable, and the bright golden-rod-colored highlights throughout the site only reinforce its modernity.

Marketing companies like Luxus (Figure 3-125) are also doing great things with their websites. Luxus incorporates a slideshow into their header that showcases statistics about their employees. Some are directly related to their business (the number of Twitter followers they have, or the number of emails received per minute), whereas others are more lighthearted (such as how many liters of milk they've drunk, or how many pairs of sneakers they own). But it's a nice touch that humanizes the company and adds a sense of familiarity.

Law firms used to be the leaders in stodgy, boring websites. Not anymore, thanks to Springhouse Solicitors (Figure 3-134). Their website is fresh, modern, and hasn't a hint of corporate color schemes anywhere. The use of a hummingbird graphic, placed prominently on its home page, further sets it apart from others in the industry.

The designs featured here often approach the typical corporate website in a very atypical way. Study how they've broken with tradition, in terms of overall design choices and the individual elements used, paying special attention to *why* those choices worked. Then consider how you could apply similar design ideas to your own projects.

Figure 3-119
Source: http://www.hunters.co.nz/wine-shop/ © Hunters Wine (NZ) Inc.

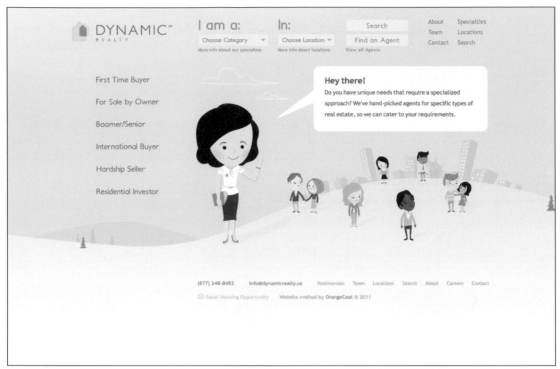

Figure 3-120
Source: http://www.dynamicrealty.us © Dynamic Realty

Figure 3-121
Source: http://graystone-inc.com © Graystone
Construction & Remodeling, Inc., site design
by Frank McClung, DrawingonthePromises.com

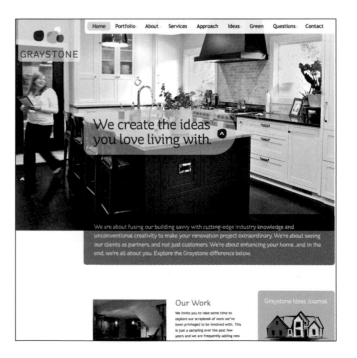

Figure 3-122
Source: http://harmonyrepublic.com © Harmony Republic

Figure 3-123
Source: http://www.infinvision.com © InfinVision Ltd.

Figure 3-124
Source: http://www.bluecadet.com © Bluecadet

Figure 3-125
Source: http://luxus.fi © Luxus

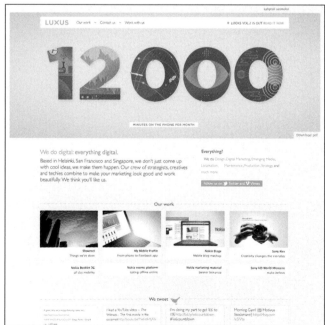

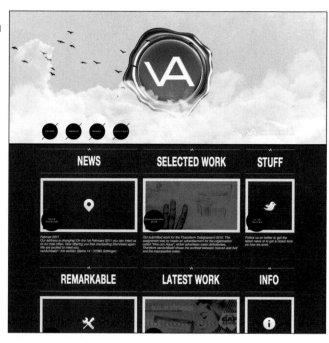

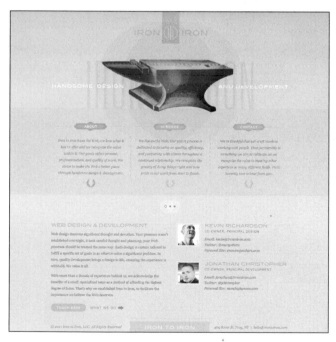

Figure 3-128

Source: http://www.wearefixel.com © Fixel

Figure 3-129

Source: http://www.iwc.com © IWC Schaffhausen

Figure 3-130
Source: http://www.woodinvillewhiskeyco.com © Woodinville
Whiskey Co.

Figure 3-131
Source: http://twogiraffes.com © Two Giraffes

Figure 3-132
Source: http://jaxvineyards.com © Jax Vineyards

Figure 3-133
Source: http://www.artofkinetik.com © Art of Kinetik

Figure 3-134
Source: http://springhouselaw.com © Springhouse Solicitors

Figure 3-135
Source: http://brokersdirect.com © Brokers Direct

Figure 3-136
Source: http://www.hurcoind.com © Hurco Design &
Manufacturing

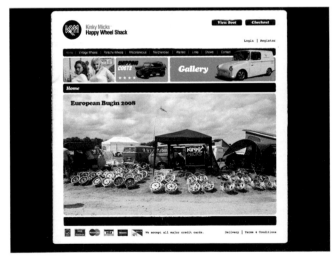

Figure 3-137
Source: http://kinkymicks.com © Kinky Micks

PORTFOLIOS

There are generally two schools of thought when it comes to portfolio design. First are the designers who feel the portfolio design itself should act as a part of the portfolio, further showing off the artistic or design skills of the site owner. The second opinion is that a portfolio design should simply fade into the background, placing the emphasis squarely on the work being featured.

In either case, the design of a portfolio speaks volumes about the artist or designer it belongs to. A poorly designed portfolio (even for someone who isn't a web designer) screams amateur, and will make visitors to the site doubt the artist's or designer's abilities.

The main challenge that comes with designing a portfolio site is to make a bunch of potentially disparate pieces blend together into a cohesive whole. In most cases, an artist's or designer's work is going to be varied, and yet the portfolio has to make it all look like it came from the same person. Often easier said than done.

The portfolio of P.A. Rochat (Figure 3-138) is a great example of using common elements to tie together a ton of varied work. By using consistent borders (reminiscent of Polaroid snapshots) for all of the work showcased, and a neutral background, the entire thing takes on a very polished, consistent look.

The portfolio of Polyester Studio (Figure 3-150) takes a more boldly graphic approach. They use bright red and green to set apart the print work from the motion work. The result is stunning, and makes it easy for visitors to find examples of exactly the kind of work they're looking for.

In addition to the design considerations outlined already, look at whether each of the portfolio sites in this section act as an additional piece of the portfolio, or simply as a neutral backdrop.

Figure 3-138
Source: http://www.parochat.ch © P.A. Rochat

Figure 3-139
Source: http://www.skodesignlab.com © Sko Design Lab

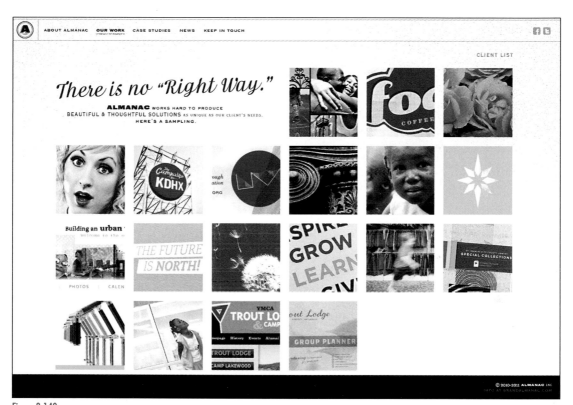

Figure 3-140

Source: http://www.brandalmanac.com/our-work/ © Almanac, Inc.

Figure 3-141

Source: http://www.neverendesign.com © Never End Design

Figure 3-142

Source: http://work.brizk.com © Brizk

Figure 3-143
Source: http://www.gregponchak.com © Greg Ponchak

Figure 3-144
Source: http://pierrickcalvez.com © Pierrick Calvez

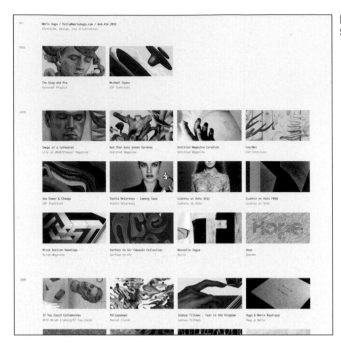

Figure 3-145
Source: http://mariohugo.com © Mario Hugo

Figure 3-146
Source: http://phantomcitycreative.com/?page_id=9 © Phantom City Creative

Figure 3-147

Source: http://www.dtelepathy.com/our-projects © Digital Telepathy

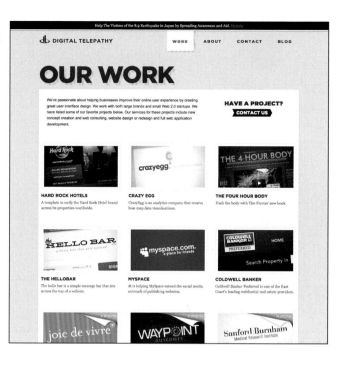

Figure 3-148

Source: http://adashofmoxie.com/d-page.php © A Dash of Moxie

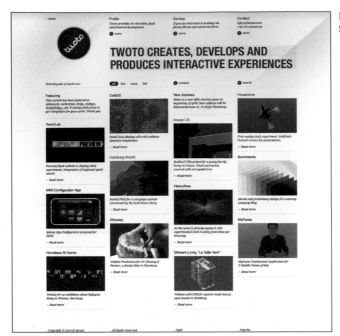

Figure 3-149
Source: http://www.twoto.com © Twoto

Figure 3-150
Source: http://www.polyesterstudio.com © Polyester Studio

Figure 3-151
Source: http://www.colinmckinney.co.uk © Colin McKinney

Figure 3-152
Source: http://www.bradlangdon.co.uk © Brad Langdon

Figure 3-155
Source: http://www.pixelot.de © Paul Schneider

Figure 3-156
Source: http://shellycooperdesign.com © Shelly Cooper

EVENT AND COMMUNITY SITES

Event and community websites often overlap (in that many communities offer events, and many events have communities grow around them). It's important that both types of sites make visitors feel at home, and like they're a part of something.

The best event and community sites make it easy to see the benefits in signing up or attending. They make visitors want to be a part of what it is they're offering, and in that way they're somewhat similar to e-commerce sites. They often showcase event and community sponsors, too, and need to do so in a way that doesn't clutter up the site or make it look like one giant advertisement.

Event sites also have to do double-duty, often serving as a recap site once the event has taken place. This can spur interest for future events, and often acts as a community builder and sales tool.

The Confab site (Figure 3-159) showcases all the important information an event site should contain: the date and place, who the prominent speakers are, and what the conference is about. It's all done in a clean, modern layout that makes information easy to find. They also do a great job of incorporating sponsor logos without cluttering up the home page.

The 99% Conference website (Figure 3-165) is actually a part of the larger 99% site. The conference page itself, though, has a great layout that presents all the pertinent information any visitor would want to know. It also fits seamlessly into the rest of the site, while still maintaining its own style, such as the dark background when the rest of the site has a white background.

When looking at the designs featured in this section, pay close attention to the way information is presented to the different types of likely visitors (vendors, attendees, sponsors, and so on), as well as the individual design details that reinforce the mood and purpose of the event or conference.

Figure 3-157
Source: http://en.tis-home.com © Tokyo Illustrators Society

Figure 3-158
Source: http://www.partyfortheparks.com © Charleston Parks
Conservancy

Figure 3-159
Source: http://www.confab2011.com © CONFAB. Designed by Sean Tubridy

Figure 3-160
Source: http://newadventuresconf.com © Simon Collison & New Adventures

Figure 3-161
Source: http://futureofwebapps.com/las-vegas-2011/
© Carson Systems Ltd.

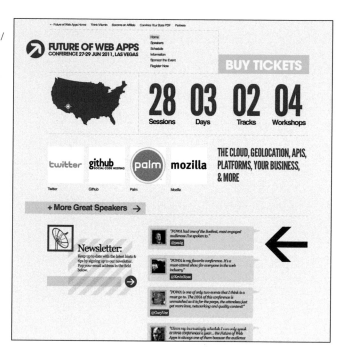

Figure 3-162
Source: http://glasshouseconversations.org © 2010 National Trust for Historic Preservation and The Philip Johnson Glass House

Figure 3-163

Source: http://www.semipermanent.com © Semi-Permanent

Figure 3-164

Source: http://sasquatchfestival.com © Sasquatch Festival

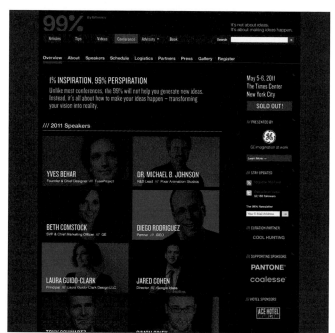

Figure 3-165
Source: http://the99percent.com/conference © Behance, LLC

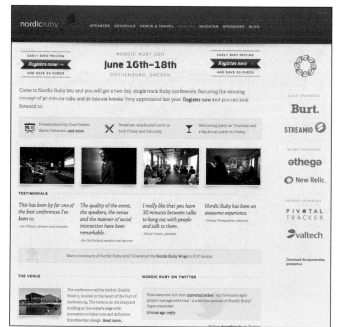

Figure 3-166
Source: http://www.nordicrugby.org © Elabs AB

Figure 3-167
Source: http://conference.cognitivecities.com
© CognitiveCities.com

PERSONAL AND PROFESSIONAL

There's a lot of overlap between personal and professional websites these days, especially among the design and social media communities. Because of that, there's a wide array of design styles present in these kinds of websites. The only thing they really all have in common is that they focus on an individual (or occasionally a couple or family).

Think about why someone would want to visit your personal or professional website. In most cases, it's something they'll visit because they've seen the person's name elsewhere, and have either followed a link or searched for the person's name. Because of this, it's important that a personal site immediately indicate to the new visitor that they've reached the correct place (and the correct person).

Beyond that, though, there's a lot of room for a person's personality to really shine through. Even with professional websites, personality is important, and is what sets one site, and one person, apart from the next.

As a photographer, it makes sense that Kimberly Knight's personal site (Figure 1-170) features a photo of herself as the background. The simple layout, short bio, and social media links round things out nicely.

A photograph on a personal website also allows the audience to connect with the person behind the site in a much more intimate way. It's not just a name that you're familiar with, it's a face. Photographs offer a better connection to be established between the individual's minds (and the ideas they speak of on their sites) and those of the audience (who read the ideas).

Cat Townsend's professional site (Figure 3-173) is a great example of this kind of site. The layout is simple but employs a Who/What/How/Why/Where organizational structure that's unexpected but easy to use.

Personal blogs built around a theme, including those for couples or families, are growing in popularity, and really fit into both the blog and personal site categories. Our Swiss Life (Figure 3-176) is one such blog. The header design is particularly interesting, while the sidebar prominently featuring the authors is a nice touch.

Personal sites often give designers a lot more leeway in how to approach the design. The main purpose of any personal site is that it reflect the personality of the individual it represents. Consider the impression each of the sites in this section give in regard to the person they're for.

Figure 3-168
Source: http://rainypixels.com © Nishant Kothary

Figure 3-169
Source: http://about.me/stephanie_adams © Stephanie Adams

Figure 3-170
Source: http://about.me/knightlight © Kimberly Knight

Figure 3-171
Source: http://ma.tt © Matt Mullenweg

Figure 3-172
Source: http://www.johannalenander.com © Johanna Lenander

Figure 3-173
Source: http://www.notpretty.net/who.html © Not Pretty Ltd.

Figure 3-174
Source: http://www.chrisglass.com © Chris Glass

Figure 3-175
Source: http://bigamericannight.com © James A. Reeves

Figure 3-176
Source: http://www.ourswisslife.com © Andrew McClintock &
Kathryn Cornelius

Figure 3-177
Source: http://strangenative.com © Russ Maschmeyer

Figure 3-178
Source: http://www.sethgodin.com/sg/ © Seth Godin

Figure 3-179
Source: http://iamgarth.com © Garth Humbert

Figure 3-180
Source: http://about.me/desombra © Ray DeSombra

Figure 3-181
Source: http://dontthrowbatteries.com © Brad Dunn

Figure 3-182
Source: http://about.me/maggie © Maggie Mason

Figure 3-183
Source: http://about.me/lisabettany © Lisa Bettany

DRAWING INSPIRATION BY INDUSTRY

There are hundreds of industries out there, and it would be kind of ridiculous to try to tackle them all in one book (let alone part of one chapter). So instead, lets look at some of the more common industries, and some of the more challenging.

There are certain design conventions within many industries. There are also certain require-ments that different industry sites need to have, due to the nature of their businesses. Studying sites within the industry you're designing for is one way to get an idea of what types of sites are expected. Just don't be afraid to try new things.

HOSPITALITY

As a general rule, sites for the hospitality industry need to be inviting to whatever demographic you or your client is targeting. For a luxury hotel near a business district, for instance, the site might need to appeal to wealthy professionals. That site is going to have a much different look and feel than a restaurant that's aimed at family diners, or a bar aimed at single 20-somethings.

Beyond appealing to the specific market of your client, most hospitality sites also need to incorporate things like an accommodations listing or menu, a map or directions, rates, and similar information. A restaurant website is probably going to want to include plenty of images of their food, while a hotel site might include pictures of the view, the neighborhood, or individual rooms.

The website for Fish in Charleston, SC (Figure 3-184) is a great example of a site that clearly emphasizes the food the restaurant has to offer. They also place links to their menu prominently, and include their hours right on the home page. Links to directions and to make reservations are also easy to find. The entire site is elegant, and obviously aimed at a higher-end clientele.

The Ace Hotel's website (Figure 3-190) is obviously aimed at hipsters and 20-somethings. The site uses an unconventional layout, but is still easy to navigate and includes links to important information (like rates and reservations) in a logical place.

The Twelve Restaurant & Lounge Bar's website (Figure 3-194) has an understated sophistication that is likely to appeal to younger professionals. Its home page features a prominent image of the food, as well as links to other information, like the menu, the team, and special offers. It's elegant and simple, while still being visually interesting.

The sites featured in this section are all excellent examples of how a hospitality site needs to directly appeal to its target demographic, whatever that might be. Pay close attention to how the details of the designs reinforce the mood and style each site portrays.

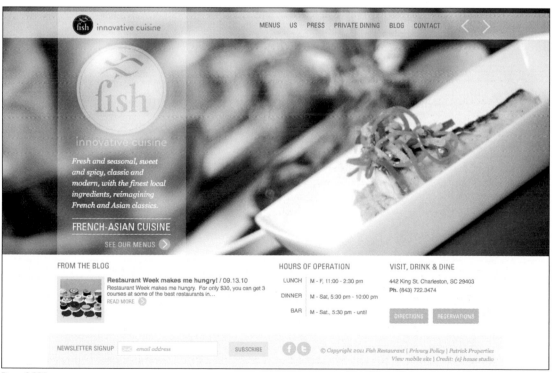

Figure 3-184
Source: http://www.fishrestaurantcharleston.com © Fish Restaurant

Figure 3-185
Source: http://www.eatatfig.com © FIG Restaurant

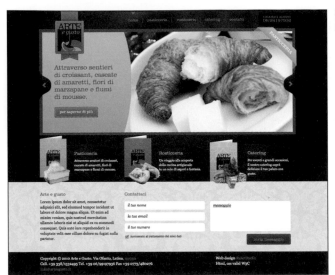

Figure 3-189
Source: http://www.arteegusto.it © Arte e Gusto

Figure 3-190
Source: http://www.acehotel.com/seattle © Ace Hotel

Figure 3-191
Source: http://www.culinariafoodandwine.com/ © Culinaria.
Designed by Jeff Immer, Biklops Design

Figure 3-196
Source: http://www.vedatakeout.com © Veda Fine Indian Takeout Inc.

Figure 3-197
Source: http://www.pizzaexpress.com © Pizza Express

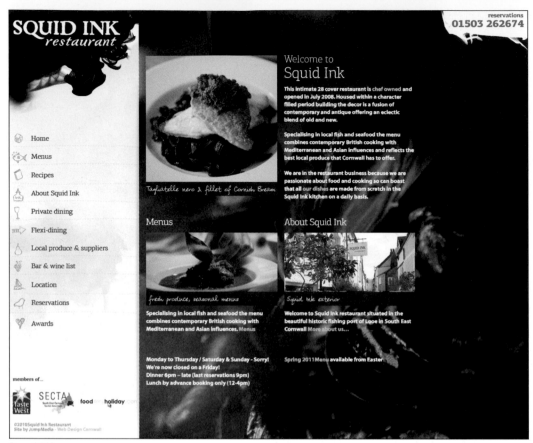

Figure 3-198

Source: http://www.squid-ink.biz © Squid Ink Restaurant

Figure 3-199

Source: http://thebalsams.com © The Balsams Grand Resort
Hotel

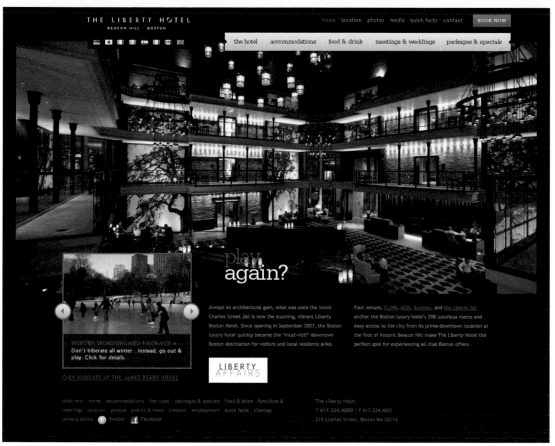

Figure 3-200

Source: http://libertyhotel.com © The Liberty Hotel

Figure 3-201

Source: http://vancouverclub.ca © Vancouver Club. Designed by Andrew Simpson and Adam Bognar, The Still Brandworks

ARTS AND ENTERTAINMENT

There's a lot of creative freedom among some sites within the arts and entertainment industries. Artists in particular often like to have more avant-garde sites, as an extension of their creativity and to place themselves in stark contrast to the perceived dryness and rigidity of corporate design. Other parts of the entertainment industry (such as record labels and production companies), though, adhere to more conservative site designs for the most part.

Sites for these industries need to adhere to the principles of good design while still offering some hint at creativity. It's a difficult line for many designers to walk, although the designs here should give you some ideas.

The design for Big Five Glories (Figure 3-203) would be equally at home for a production company as it is for this classic movie website. The dark color scheme and simple layout put the emphasis on the content, while the prominent header and tag line make it clear what the site is all about. It's sophisticated and well organized, and works very well for the content it provides.

The site for Atlantic Records (Figure 3-205) is modern and uses a strong grid layout. It's a site design that should appeal to a wide demographic, which is important for a company like Atlantic. The navigation is well-designed, making it easy to find various information, and content on the home page is made to be updated regularly, which should help keep visitors coming back.

The Rekkiabilly website (Figure 3-218) reflects the band's attitude and music well. It gives visitors an idea of what their music is probably going to sound like before they ever listen to a clip. It's also got great organization and displays the most important information (tour dates, the newsletter sign-up form, and merchandise) prominently.

Art and entertainment websites like those featured here are often hugely creative in their own right. Look to the unconventional approaches some of the sites in this section have taken, as well as how they place emphasis on the content rather than just the design.

Figure 3-202
Source: http://www.foxclassics.com.au © FOXTEL
MANAGEMENT PTY LIMITED

Figure 3-203
Source: http://www.bigfiveglories.com © Big Five Glories

Figure 3-204
Source: http://heypapalegend.com © HeyPapaLegend Studios

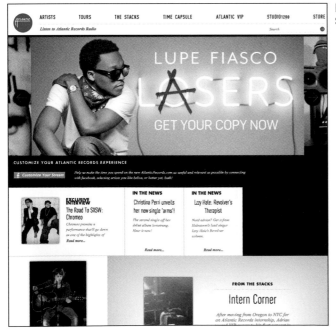

Figure 3-205
Source: http://atlanticrecords.com © Atlantic Records

Figure 3-206
Source: http://www.bullyentertainment.com © Bully!
Entertainment

Figure 3-207
Source: http://www.futurefilmfestival.org/intl © Future Film
Festival

Figure 3-208

Source: http://www.nonesuch.com © Nonesuch Records

Figure 3-209

Source: http://www.rocketclub.info © Rocket Club

Figure 3-210
Source: http://tokyopoliceclub.com/home/ © The Tokyo Police Club

Figure 3-211
Source: http://hellokavita.net © Hello Kavita

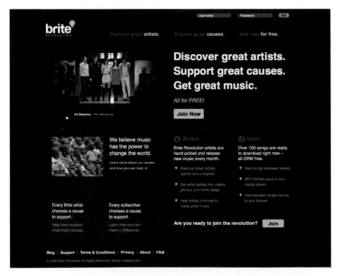

Figure 3-214
Source: http://www.picmixstore.com © Callum Chapman

Figure 3-215
Source: http://moblues.org © Mo Blues

Figure 3-216
Source: http://ronlewhorn.com © Ronlewhorn

Figure 3-217
Source: http://youzee.com © Youzee

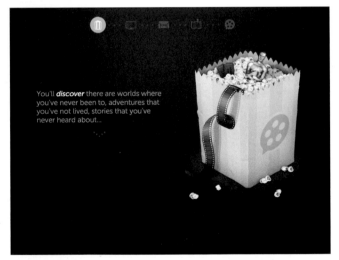

Figure 3-218
Source: http://www.rekkiabilly.com © Rekkiabilly

Figure 3-219
Source: http://svencurth.com. Designed
by Jim Gunardson

APPS AND SOFTWARE

Although the overall app industry has a wide variety of customers, individual app websites generally cater to very specific demographics. Because of this ability to pinpoint their ideal visitor, designers can often be more secure in knowing that a particular design will work well. And that means they can sometimes be much more creative and try things that might not go over well on other sites.

Software companies sometimes need to have sites with slightly more mass appeal, but they still usually target one group of consumers pretty exclusively. The good news about these kinds of sites is that the companies usually know exactly who their target demographic is, and they're generally more tech-savvy than a lot of other clients you might have.

One thing to keep in mind is that the complexity of an app site should mirror the complexity and user level of the app or software itself. Software aimed at casual users should have simpler websites than those aimed at more advanced users. Keep in mind, though, that consumers who buy software online are generally more tech-savvy than your average Internet user.

The website for Open Public (Figure 3-220) has a very traditional style, reminiscent of government websites (but much better designed than the vast majority of them), which fits since it's aimed at governments. The subtle motifs in the graphics are reminiscent of money or official certificates, which adds polish and a sense of order, quality, and reliability to the overall design.

Postmark's website (Figure 2-227) is eye-catching, thanks in no small part to the bright yellow header. Despite the fact that it's aimed primarily at developers, it has a very consumer-friendly design. The site is easy to navigate and puts the most important information (including pricing) right on the home page.

The website for Mobile Roadie (Figure 2-232) has a clean, dark design that's likely to appeal to a wide demographic. Since Mobile Roadie is a platform rather than a specific app, that's important in this case. They prominently feature news on the home page, as well as show-casing some of their users. The blue for the call-to-action button is a surprising choice (green would be the more obvious choice, especially with the purple background), but it works well here, at least in part due to the fresh and modern mood it portrays.

When looking at the designs included here, pay attention to how the mood of the site directly relates to the purpose and mood of the software or app being offered, as well as user interface similarities between the two.

Figure 3-220
Source: http://www.openpublicapp.com © Phase2 Technology

Figure 3-221
Source: http://www.locomotivecms.com © NoCoffee. Designed by Sacha Greif

Figure 3-222
Source: http://www.alfredapp.com © Running with Crayons, Ltd.

Figure 3-223
Source: http://www.postbox-inc.com © Postbox, Inc.

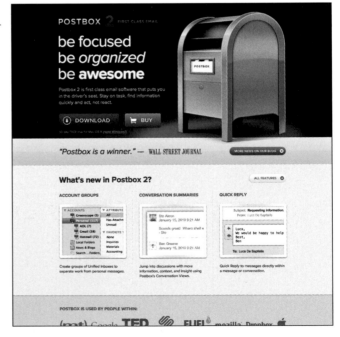

Figure 3-224
Source: http://www.unlocking.com © UniquePhones, Inc.
Design by Panduka Senaka

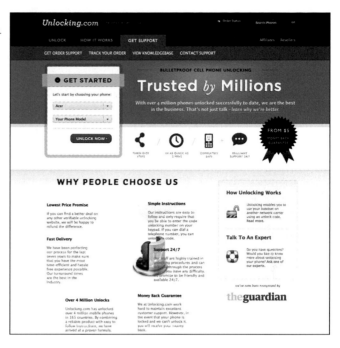

Figure 3-225
Source: http://www.readyforzero.com © Ready for Zero

Figure 3-226
Source: http://momentoapp.com © d3i Ltd.

Figure 3-227
Source: http://postmarkapp.com © Wildbit LLC

Figure 3-228
Source: http://www.zennaware.com/cornerstone/index.php
© Zennaware

Figure 3-229
Source: http://supermegaultragroovy.com/products/Capo/
© SuperMegaUltraGroovy

Figure 3-230
Source: http://itsworkable.com/home © Peritus Media

Figure 3-231
Source: http://www.helpscout.net © Brightwurks

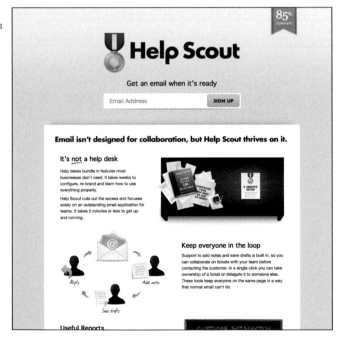

Figure 3-232
Source: http://www.mobileroadie.com © Mobile Roadie, LLC

Figure 3-233
Source: http://www.tapparatus.com/isaidwhat/ © Tapparatus

Figure 3-234
Source: http://www.delibarapp.com © Shiny Frog

Figure 3-235
Source: http://feedafever.com © Shaun Inman

Figure 3-236
Source: http://pulseapp.com © Pulseapp.com

Figure 3-237
Source: http://www.theresumator.com © The Resumator

Figure 3-238
Source: http://newsberry.com © Newsberry

Figure 3-238
Source: http://newsberry.com © Newsberry

Figure 3-239
Source: http://munch5aday.com © MeYou Health, LLC

TECHNOLOGY

The technology industry is huge, and to some extent, very disjointed. There are tons of different companies that fall under the heading "technology," and there's very little commonality between many of them.

The lack of continuity can make it difficult to come up with ideas for technology sites. But if you look long enough, you'll find that there are two basic camps when it comes to tech site design. The first camp creates overtly "techy" sites: they're clean, polished, and glossy, often with lots of bells and whistles.

The other camp takes a completely opposite approach. Plug in different content and you'd never know the site was originally designed for a tech company. It's an interesting approach, and one that can make for some very memorable sites.

The Host Bacon site (Figure 3-240) falls into the second camp. Beige is generally the last color you'd think of for a tech site, and the typeface used is also decidedly un-techy. But combined with the name of the company, the overall design works. And it makes for a very memorable user experience.

TestingScrum's site (Figure 3-246) falls somewhere in between. It looks techy enough once you know it's a technology site, but if you changed out the content it would still work in a lot of industries. The design itself is bold and well planned, with some unexpected choices (including the URL bar in the middle of the screen that doubles as a content divider).

On the opposite end of the spectrum, the site for OpenDNS (Figure 3-250) is decidedly techy. It just wouldn't work outside the technology sector. The orange and dark gray header is modern and bold, and the graphics on the site back up that feeling.

Look at the approach taken by each site in this section, and whether they've decided to embrace the technology image of their company or opt for a less conventional and more people-oriented design that would be perfectly at home outside the technology industry.

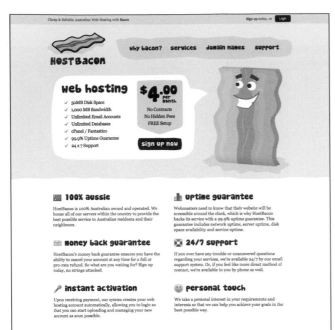

Figure 3-240
Source: http://hostbacon.com.au © Vic Olbromski, HostBacon

Figure 3-241
Source: http://www.macalicious.com © Macalicious

Figure 3-244

Source: http://thenextweb.com © The Next Web

Figure 3-245

Source: http://webstandardssherpa.com. Used with permission from the Web Standards Project

Figure 3-246
Source: http://www.testingscrum.com © TestingScrum

Figure 3-247
Source: http://www.medialoot.com © MediaLoot, Inc. Designed by Mason Hipp

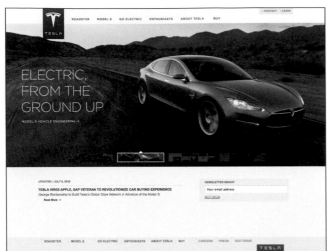

Figure 3-248
Source: http://www.teslamotors.com © Tesla Motors

Figure 3-249
Source: http://www.boxee.tv © Boxee, Inc.

Figure 3-250
Source: http://www.opendns.com © OpenDNS

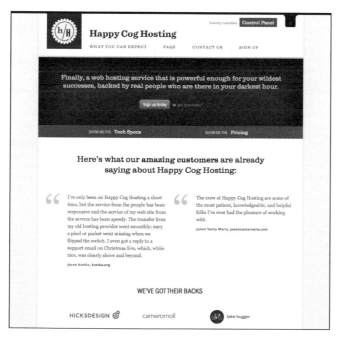

Figure 3-251
Source: http://happycoghosting.com © Happy Cog

FASHION

The fashion industry is another sector that has a huge amount of variety. Falling under the "fashion" umbrella is everything from haute couture to casual, everyday wear. To an extent, fashion company websites often resemble portfolios. Fashion blogs are often minimalist in appearance, with the emphasis placed squarely on the images the site features. Fashion retailers run the gamut of e-commerce site styles.

The key to remember with many fashion sites is that they're another form of art. Creativity is generally embraced, and many fashion-forward companies will have no problem trying something unconventional. But remember, too, that fashion is big business, and there's often a lot of money at stake, especially for the larger companies. A corporate mindset is still important.

Marie Saint Pierre's website (Figure 3-255) is a great example of a designer website. The video header that takes up the majority of the screen showcases the designer's work, while the rest of the site is kept very simple.

The organizational structure of the Every Guyed blog (Figure 3-263) showcases just how complex the fashion industry can be. But it's handled beautifully here, with a grid-style layout and simple color scheme.

The mood of a fashion website is hugely important when it comes to reinforcing the brand the site represents. Above all else, the mood and style of the design can make or break the site. Pay close attention to how the sites included here incorporate details that reinforce the site's brand.

Figure 3-252
Source: http://www.farfetch.com © Farfetch.com

Figure 3-253
Source: http://www.nylonmag.com © Nylon Holding, Inc.

Figure 3-254
Source: http://www.bokicabo.com/en/03/ © BokicaBo

Figure 3-255
Source: http://www.mariesaintpierre.com/en © Marie Saint Pierre. Created by www.toxa.ca and www.leloi.ca

Figure 3-256
Source: http://www.madeforyoubyarms.com © Arms

Figure 3-257
Source: http://www.thecoveteur.com © The Coveteur

Figure 3-258
Source: http://www.mikkatmarket.com © Mikkat Market

Figure 3-259
Source: http://www.monki.com © Monki

Figure 3-260
Source: http://www.lovelybride.com/blog/index.
php/2011/03/11/one-great-dress-mother-knows-best/
© Lovey Bride. Designed by Sara Ramsey

Figure 3-261
Source: http://whatiwore.tumblr.com © Jessica Quirk

Figure 3-262
Source: http://www.boraaksu.com © Bora Aksu

Figure 3-263
Source: http://everyguyed.com © Every Guyed

Figure 3-264
Source: http://dressir.com © Dressir.com

Figure 3-265

Source: http://www.japanesestreets.com © Japanese Streets

Figure 3-266

Source: http://www.modcloth.com © ModCloth

Figure 3-267
Source: http://www.stewartbrown.com © Stewart+Brown

Figure 3-268
Source: http://thelocals.dk © The Locals

Figure 3-269
Source: http://www.cfan-designs.com © C/Fan

LITERATURE AND BOOKS

Publishing and book-related websites are notoriously poorly designed in the vast majority of cases. It's not just the visuals, either. They often suffer from serious usability issues, as well as poor organizational structures.

There are some true shining gems out there, though, and they're becoming more common as authors, booksellers, publishers, and literary magazines recognize the importance of a web presence.

Similar to blogs and magazine sites, it's important for most book and literary sites to have excellent typography and content organization. Beyond that, though, there's a lot of room for creativity and experimentation in design.

The Wisdom of Bees is one example of a great book website (Figure 3-270). The bold, yellow header and bee graphics fit perfectly with the overall theme of the book, and navigation links are placed prominently. The call-to-action buttons (one to buy the book and one to sign up for alerts) are also well-designed. Black for the primary call-to-action works in this case, because it's used so sparingly throughout the rest of the design and sits in stark contrast to the yellow and white.

The website for literary journal n+1 (Figure 3-272) is a shining example of a modern, well-designed literary website. The organization of the home page is outstanding, as is the readability of the site's typography. The tan background and red-orange accents throughout the site are sophisticated yet modern.

The Millions (Figure 3-279) is a great example of a book-related site that needs to organize a lot of content that changes on a regular basis. The simple grid layout, and black and white color scheme create a site that's easy to navigate while also being sophisticated. The orange logo and dark red accents throughout the site add necessary extra punches of color and keep the design from being boring.

The mood and general style of the sites here is as varied as the books, magazines, and comics they represent. Pay close attention to how the design details used reinforce the content of the sites, and how they sometimes use unexpected choices to differentiate themselves from similar sites.

Figure 3-270
Source: http://www.thewisdomofbees.com
© Michael O'Malley, Ph.D.

Figure 3-271
Source: http://www.readability.com © Readability, LLC

Figure 3-272
Source: http://nplusonemag.com © n+1 Foundation

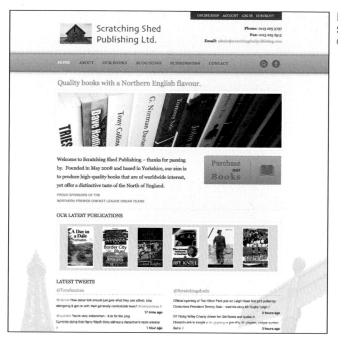

Figure 3-273
Source: http://www.scratchingshedpublishing.co.uk
© Scratching Shed Publishing Ltd.

Figure 3-274
Source: http://apps.forgottencolours.com © Play Attitude

Figure 3-275
Source: http://www.greenboathouse.com © Greenboathouse
Press

Figure 3-276
Source: http://fictionwritersreview.com © Fiction Writers
Review. Site design by Marissa Perry

Figure 3-277
Source: http://www.michiganquarterlyreview.com © Michigan Quarterly Review

Figure 3-278
Source: http://www.theparisreview.org © The Paris Review

Figure 3-279
Source: http://www.themillions.com © The Millions

Figure 3-280
Source: http://www.guysread.com © Guys Read

Figure 3-281
Source: http://www.book-by-its-cover.com © Julia Rothman

Figure 3-282
Source: http://bookcoverarchive.com © The Book Cover Archive

Figure 3-283
Source: http://www.fiell.com/page/our-books © Fiell Publishing.
Site designed by Stylo Design

Figure 3-284
Source: http://communitybookstore.net © The Community
Bookstore

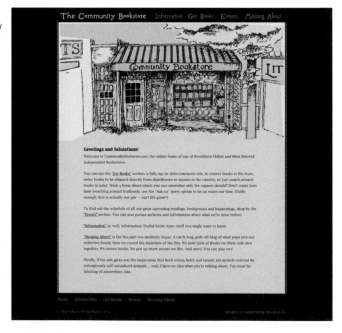

Figure 3-285
Source: http://bergenstreetcomics.com © Bergen Street Comics

Figure 3-286
Source: http://www.powerhousearena.com © The Powerhouse Arena

Figure 3-287
Source: http://www.strandbooks.com © Strand Book Store

Figure 3-288
Source: http://www.mcnallyjackson.com © McNally Jackson
Books

CONCLUSION

Regardless of what kind of site you're designing, there are likely designs already present online that you can draw inspiration from. Remember, there are no truly new ideas, and everything has likely been done before. Make the design your own in the way that you combine elements and the overall feel of the finished product, rather than trying to invent something completely unique.

Rarely are two clients and their problems ever the same, so understanding both and deriving a solution directly from each, while aiming squarely at the audience, helps you to take all the inspiration knocking around in your head and turn it into something wonderful.

OTHER DESIGNS

4

WEBSITES AREN'T THE only designs to draw inspiration from. There's a whole world of other designs out there that can be drawn upon to inspire your projects. Everything from graphic design to architecture to product design can be studied for new perspective on tackling age-old design challenges.

Just taking a look around your workspace or out your office window is likely to offer up dozens of potential sources of inspiration, if you'll only learn to look at things that way. Everything from the color of something to the shape of it can inspire you. The way the sunlight glints off a surface can be just as inspiring as looking at a website similar to the one you're trying to design (if not more so).

One of the greatest things about more indirect inspiration like the examples here is that you can show the same images or objects to ten different designers and you'll likely get ten very different interpretations, some of which would bear little resemblance to the original inspiration. The same can't generally be said for website designs that serve as inspiration.

GRAPHIC DESIGN

The world of graphic design has at least as much variation as web design, and has been around a lot longer. Print design alone has a varied history that spans back to the invention of the printing press, invented by Johann Gutenberg around 1440. Just studying designs from the past century could give you enough potential inspiration to last your entire career.

Consider looking at print layouts for alternative ideas on organization and web layout, as well as ideas for things like color schemes or textures. Regardless of where you live, you likely have access to magazines, books, packaging, advertisements, and more great examples of graphic designs.

PRINT DESIGN

Good design is good design; the principles are often the same in spite of the medium in which they are executed. Looking at print design can help a designer understand contrast, scale, texture, and on and on. Looking at history also allows one to see how styles and fashion and other ideas have been executed—this is the real value of printed design.

Print design is a great place to find inspiration for how to structure your website designs. It often contains examples of excellent typography, with an emphasis on readability. Strong imagery is often present, as well.

There are magazines and books out there for virtually every subject and industry, so there's almost certainly a magazine related to the industry you're designing for. But don't limit yourself to just that industry; look across consumer and trade titles for original ideas that might not have been successfully tried on the web before.

Advertisements in print publications can also be a wealth of possible inspiration. There have been print ads since the early days of newspapers. Open just about any magazine or newspaper and you'll find dozens of them. Like all designs, though, some are better than others.

Print ads are great for finding inspiration for things like color schemes or headline styles. Sometimes they're shining examples of typography and layout, although their graphics can sometimes be too complex to translate well to the web.

The world of print design is inhabited by some of the best designers, copywriters, photographers, and illustrators in the world because ROI demands it. They're a great example of how to grab someone's attention and tell a story in only a second. Powerful ideas and techniques can be gleamed from print layouts and advertising.

The asymmetrical columns, minimalist layout, and extravagant drop cap of the Nylon magazine layout in Figure 4-3 could easily be adapted to a blog or other text-heavy site.

The ad in Figure 4-10 has great texture and use of negative space that would be right at home on the web. The color scheme is also great, and could easily be adapted.

The ad in Figure 4-17, on the other hand, has not only a great layout that could be adapted, but also wonderful typography. It shows just what can be done with a single typeface in a variety of weights and styles.

The other print designs in this section are rife with ideas for big-picture elements like focus, mood, and layout, as well as details like typography.

Figure 4-1
Source: Juxtapoz Magazine © High Speed Productions

Figure 4-2
Source: Nylon © Nylon Holding, Inc.

few years ago, Karen Elson started locking herself in her bedroom closet. Armed with a guitar and laptop, the crimson-haired model picked out songs and typed up lyrics, working as quietly as possible so her husband, Jack White, wouldn't hear. But her plan failed. White started eavesdropping and then (sweetly) demanding that she open the door. "Let me hear these songs for real," he pleaded. "Stop hiding them." Finally, she emerged and worked up the courage to play him "Mouths to Feed," a mournful, dust-bowl ballad steeped in Steinbeck-style imagery and heartache. "I had to really push that devil off my shoulder and get over myself," Elson says.

It's a good thing she did. White, not surprisingly, loved the song, which is now the last track on Elson's debut album, *The Ghost Who Walks*, a gorgeous collection of bluesy folk songs and haunting Appalachian dirges that White produced. "The record is directly born from the fact that I moved to Nashville and had children and just had time to really sit back and reflect," says Elson, who has been walking runways for designers like Marc Jacobs and John Paul Gaultier since she was 16. As for the reason an English lass found herself drawn to country stylings, pedal steel, and fiddles? "It's in the water here," she says in a delicate British accent.

This isn't Elson's first foray into music. Growing up outside of Manchester, England, she had "teenage dreams of wanting to sing" and joined a salsa group in high school. In 2004, when she was living in New York City, she co-founded the Citizens Band, a political cabaret collective that ultimately made her believe in herself as a performer. "It helped me get over the model-slash-dot dot dot stigma," she says. "I felt plagued by that for some time."

Though Elson says recording *The Ghost Who Walks* wasn't always easy—"I did have a few obstacles in the way, which were basically me, myself, and I"—she couldn't be happier with the results. "It means everything to me. That fear of letting it go and having people say, 'Oh, she's a fake,' clouded me for a while. But I bit the bullet and came out the other end." Of course, her most important audience, Scarlett, four, and Henry, two, couldn't care less. "They just want me to be Mum," she says, with a laugh. "They're like, 'Bring out the bubbles and let's be silly!'"

ELLEN CARPENTER

jacket by marc jacobs.

162

Figure 4-3
Source: Echo Magazine © Echo Magazine

Figure 4-4

Source: http://raifceyhunsahin.wordpress.com © Raif Ceyhun Sahin

Figure 4-5

Source: http://www.seancomeaux.com © Sean Comeaux

Figure 4-6

Source: http://www.flickr.com © J. Kleyn

194 PART II: INSPIRING IMAGES

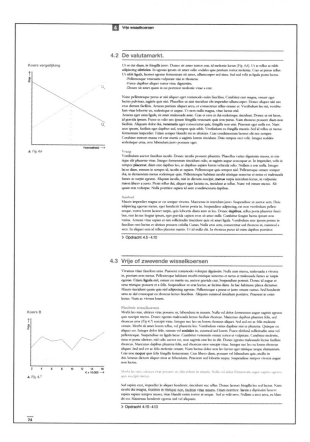

Figure 4-7
Source: http://www.flickr.com © J. Kleyn

Figure 4-8
Source: http://adsoftheworld.com © Welho

Figure 4-9

Source: http://adsoftheworld.com © Foundation abbe Pierre

Figure 4-10
Source: http://adsoftheworld.com © Visi Magazine

Figure 4-11
Source: http://adsoftheworld.com © Boutique Guitar Exchange

MARTIAN SUMMER

While the Viking experiments were redone in the hyper-arid desert of Chile, one of Peter's grad students, Doug Archer, investigated a mysterious gas release that the TEGA team saw at 300 degrees Celsius. Peter thinks it represents the moment perchlorate destroys the evidence of organics. Still more clues that Mars might indeed be covered with organic and possibly biologic material. We just can't detect it quite as easily as we originally thought.

THE FUTURE OF MARS

"He thinks he can show that there's 1-10 parts per million of organic material in the soil. Now we've got liquid water and organics," Peter says, pretending to smash his fist on the table as an exclamatory gesture. And it just gets better. Selby Cull, a student from Ray Arvidson's group, is looking into evidence that there was perchlorate all over the landing site. And maybe that will lead to showing that Perchlorate is all over Mars. She thinks she sees evidence in the some of the SSI photography.

"So even if Nilton's liquid water is just a local condition, perchlorate is probably not," Peter says with enthusiasm about ongoing discovery. "This makes this mission a real stepping stone. This is a great segue for the next Mars mission, MSL [Mars Science Laboratory]. They have a way of detecting organic material by heating and another method that doesn't use heat. We don't have proof, but we're getting closer to understanding."

LAST TANGO IN PARIS • NOTTING HILL • MUNICH • LAWRENCE OF ARABIA • LEAVING LAS VEGAS • LETTERS FROM IWO JIMA • THE BRIDGE ON THE RIVER KWAI
CITY OF GOD • MOULIN ROUGE • PHILADELPHIA • SEVEN YEARS IN TIBET • CHICAGO • PIRATES OF THE CARIBBEAN • THE LAST KING OF SCOTLAND
COMING TO AMERICA • WHAT HAPPENS IN VEGAS • FROM RUSSIA WITH LOVE • BYE BYE, BRASIL • ATLANTIC CITY • THE AFRICAN QUEEN • AMERICA, AMERICA
ATLANTIC CITY • CALIFORNIA SUITE • CAMELOT • THE CONQUEST OF EVEREST • EUROPA EUROPA • HARLAN COUNTY U.S.A. • HIROSHIMA MON AMOUR
JUDGMENT AT NUREMBERG • BRAZIL • ONCE UPON A TIME IN AMERICA • MANHATTAN • NASHVILLE • OKLAHOMA! • A PASSAGE TO INDIA • RAISING ARIZONA • SAHARA
THE THIEF OF BAGDAD • TOKYO STORY • THE TREASURE OF THE SIERRA MADRE • WOODSTOCK • LOS ANGELES CONFIDENCIAL • AN AMERICAN WEREWOLF IN LONDON
UNDER THE ROOFS OF PARIS • THE PURPLE • ROSE OF CAIRO • CARLOTA JOAQUINA, PRINCESS OF BRAZIL • HOTEL RWANDA • BERLIN: SYMPHONY OF A GREAT
CITY • THE DOCS OF NEW YORK • EUROPA 51 • THE LADY FROM SHANGHAI • STORM OVER ASIA • INDIA SONG • MISSISSIPPI: BURNING • MIRACLE IN MILAN
PARIS, TEXAS • I AM CUBA • OUT OF ROSENHEIM • BULLETS OVER BROADWAY • EUROPA • A PASSAGE TO INDIA • SANTIAGO • THE STREETS OF CASABLANCA
ON BROADWAY • NOWHERE IN AFRICA • BOWLING FOR COLUMBINE • JOURNEY TO ITALY • PERSEPOLIS • SAN FRANCISCO • TOKYO TWILIGHT • MOSCOW DOES NOT
BELIEVE IN TEARS • PARIS ASLEEP • FELLINI'S ROMA • ROSA LUXEMBURG • INDOCHINE • MOTHER INDIA • SÃO PAULO, S.A. • RAISING ARIZONA • ANNA AND
THE KING OF SIAM • THE CHINA SYNDROME • THIRTY SECONDS OVER TOKYO • WATERLOO BRIDGE • I DREAMED OF AFRICA • THE PRINCE OF EGYPT • IS PARIS
BURNING? • AN INN IN TOKYO • ABERDEEN • BATTLE OF BRITAIN • GERMANY PALE MOTHER • STALINGRAD • NEW YORK, I LOVE YOU • THE TAILOR OF PANAMA
BEVERLY HILLS COP • ROMANCE IN MANHATTAN • MIAMI VICE • PEARL HARBOR • ANNAPOLIS • U.S. MARSHALLS • GOOD MORNING, VIETNAM • CINCINNATI KID
TENNESSEE STALLION • OUT OF AFRICA • CRAZY IN ALABAMA • MYSTERY, ALASKA • BATTLE OF ALGIERS • OPERATION AMSTERDAM • SCOTT OF THE ANTARCTIC
ROAD TO BALI • THE BALTIMORE BULLET • BANGKOK DANGEROUS • BEIJING BICYCLE • WEST BEIRUT • IF IT'S TUESDAY, THIS MUST BE BELGIUM
BERLIN ALEXANDERPLATZ • SALAAM BOMBAY • FROM HELL TO BORNEO • BOSTON STRANGLER • FORT APACHE: THE BRONX • LAST EXIT TO BROOKLYN • OH CALCUTTA
SWIMMING TO CAMBODIA • CARIBBEAN MYSTERY • MAN FROM COLORADO • A CONNECTICUT YANKEE • DAKOTA INCIDENT • THINGS TO DO IN DENVER WHEN YOU'RE DEAD

THE WORLD IS INSPIRING. TRAVEL.

SHANGRI-LÁ
OPERADORA DE TURISMO
SHANGRI-LA.TUR.BR

Figure 4-14
Source: http://adsoftheworld.com © Embratur, The Brazilian Tourist Board

Figure 4-15
Source: http://adsoftheworld.com © NYC Office of Film, Theatre, and Broadcasting

Figure 4-16
Source: http://adsoftheworld.com © Black Friday Rescue League

Figure 4-17
Source: http://adsoftheworld.com © RockResorts

PRODUCT PACKAGING

Product packaging is as varied as the products it promotes. And that's exactly what product packaging is: a promotional tool. Look at the packaging that surrounds you and notice how its primary goal is always the same: to entice you to buy or consume.

This is why product packaging can be an excellent source of inspiration for e-commerce and corporate sites. Any time you're trying to sell something, there's likely a product package that's already been created that could be adapted to the web.

The packaging for DANI Soy Candles (Figure 4-18) is a great example of how minimalist packaging can be visually striking. In this case, white typography on the transparent box makes the packaging stand out from more "designed" alternatives.

If you're looking for inspiration for a vintage or grunge design, what better place to get it than something that's both retro and grungy in real life? The vintage packaging for Marvel Mystery Oil (Figure 4-29) would be a great source to draw from for a grungy or retro site with a bold color scheme and graphics.

Package designs featured here are more great sources of ideas for not only design details, but also the way content (the product) is presented (the packaging). Pay close attention to how the content and presentation interact.

Figure 4-18
Source: http://www.globalpackagegallery.com © DANI Soy Candles

Figure 4-19
Source: http://www.globalpackagegallery.com © Glucosamine
Joint Juice | Glass Packaging Institute

Figure 4-20
Source: http://www.awildsoapbar.com © A Wild Soap Bar

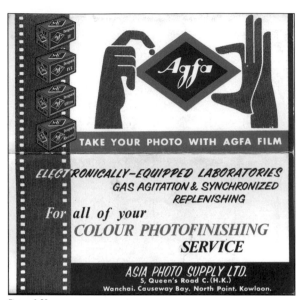

Figure 4-21
Source: http://www.littlemonkeyhands.com © AGFA

Figure 4-22
Source: http://www.globalpackagegallery.com © Iron City Brewing Company

Figure 4-23
Source: http://sorayadarwish.wordpress.com © Almarai

Figure 4-24
Source: http://www.globalpackagegallery.com © Glowelle Beauty Juice

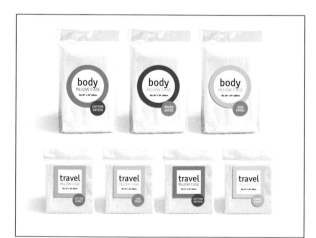

Figure 4-25
Source: http://www.globalpackagegallery.com © Beach Packaging Design

Figure 4-26
Source: http://www.globalpackagegallery.com © Glass Packaging Institute

Figure 4-27
Source: http://www.flickr.com © John Lloyd

Figure 4-28
Source: http://www.flickr.com © John Lloyd

Figure 4-29
Source: http://www.flickr.com © John Lloyd

Figure 4-30
Source: http://www.flickr.com © Vancouver Film School

ARCHITECTURE AND INTERIOR DESIGN

Graphic design may have a long and varied history, but it's nothing compared to the history of architecture around the world. Since people lived in caves tens of thousands of years ago, they've been decorating their living and working spaces. It seems to be a natural part of our makeup to want to personalize and customize the spaces we inhabit.

The beauty of drawing from architecture and interior design for your web design projects is that you're already surrounded by it. Virtually every town and every city in the entire world has at least some shining gems of architectural excellence. All you have to do is find them. And even if you can't find something in the real world to inspire you, there are millions of photos and architectural drawings available online.

EXTERIOR ARCHITECTURE

Exterior architecture is the easiest to view, because there's no need for special permission in most cases (as long as the architecture in question is visible from public land, like a road). The other great thing about exterior architecture is that there are styles out there to suit just about everyone's taste, from gothic to modern, classical to contemporary.

The red and white color scheme of the house in Figure 4-31 could easily be adapted to a website design. But look, too, to the vertical lines of the siding, and the texture of the tiled roof for even more inspiration.

The grand scale of the architecture in Figure 4-34 could inspire a formal, elegant design. The repetition and symmetry of the building could also foster ideas about pattern and balance.

The buildings in Figure 4-40 are a wealth of possible inspiration. From the curve of the roofs to the textures present throughout, there's a lot of material to draw from here.

Beyond color scheme, scale, texture, and other design details, pay attention to the mood created by the buildings included in this section and how they achieve their intended functions.

Figure 4-36
Source: http://www.flickr.com © Pedro Ribeiro Simões

Figure 4-37
Source: http://www.flickr.com © Jeremy Keith

Figure 4-38
Source: http://www.flickr.com © Pedro Ribeiro Simões

Figure 4-39
Source: http://www.flickr.com © Paul Stevenson

Figure 4-40
Source: http://www.flickr.com © TANAKA Juuyoh

Figure 4-41
Source: http://www.flickr.com © Ivan Walsh

Figure 4-42
Source: http://www.flickr.com © Toshihiro Oimatsu

Figure 4-43
Source: http://www.flickr.com © Luis Argerich

Figure 4-44
Source: http://www.flickr.com © Edyta Materka

Figure 4-45
Source: http://www.flickr.com © UggBoy UggGirl

Figure 4-46
Source: http://www.flickr.com © André Mouraux

INTERIOR ARCHITECTURE

Whereas exterior architecture is all about the public face put forth to the world, interior architecture is more about function and comfort. Examples in the real world are plentiful in public buildings, and the Internet can provide plenty of images of additional interiors.

The interior shown in Figure 4-48, for example, has a wealth of possible inspiration for you to pull from. There's great texture, a variety of shapes, great colors, and more, all from a single image. The mood alone could serve as the basis for countless designs.

In contrast to the mood of the previous example, look at Figure 4-56. There's still some great textures and shapes here, but the mood is entirely different—warm and inviting where the previous image was dark and cold.

Figure 4-60 is another great example of how interior architecture provides a wealth of possible inspiration. Here you have textures, colors, shapes, and mood to draw on.

Study the mood and purpose of the designs included in this section, in addition to the details they can inspire.

Figure 4-47
Source: http://www.flickr.com © Vincent Desjardins

Figure 4-48
Source: http://www.flickr.com © Christine Zenino

Figure 4-49
Source: http://www.flickr.com © Chad K

Figure 4-50
Source: http://www.flickr.com © Keith Tyler

Figure 4-51
Source: http://www.flickr.com © John Walker

Figure 4-52
Source: http://www.flickr.com © Jared Tarbell

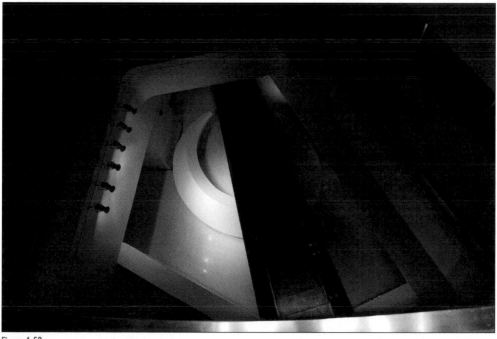

Figure 4-53
Source: http://www.flickr.com © Sakena Ali

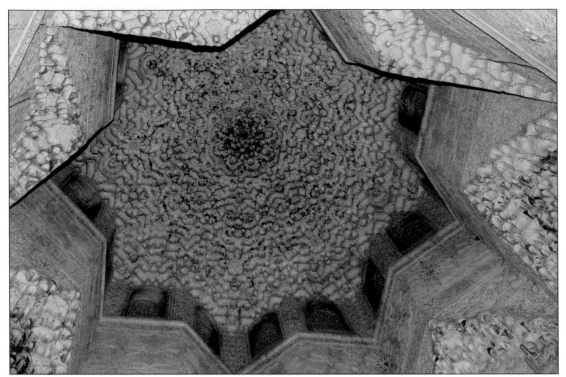

Figure 4-54
Source: http://www.flickr.com © Son of Groucho

Figure 4-55
Source: http://www.flickr.com © Nancy JonesFrancis

Figure 4-60
Source: http://www.flickr.com © Eliazar Parra Cardenas

Figure 4-61
Source: http://www.flickr.com © Chad K

Figure 4-62
Source: http://www.flickr.com © Number Six (Bill Lapp)

INTERIOR DESIGN

Whereas interior architecture focuses on the buildings, interior design focuses more on the things that inhabit those buildings. Interior design can provide a wealth of textures, colors, shapes, and patterns to adapt for your designs. Look online for images, as well as in magazines and even watch home improvement shows for inspiration.

The wealth of textures in Figure 4-64 is a gold mine for designers. There's the texture of the stone, the reflective surface of the mirror, and the texture of the antlers. There's also some great subtle color here that could be adapted into a beautiful color scheme.

Figure 4-68 is another great example of textures and colors that could be adapted into a website design. The granite countertop, copper canisters, bamboo cutting board, and wood cabinets could all be drawn from, as well as the rich, dark colors of most of the objects in the image.

Interior design is often as much about what's left out of a room as what's included. Keep that in mind when viewing the images here, and think about how what's included places emphasis on different elements and creates different moods.

Figure 4-63
Source: http://www.flickr.com © Clarkston SCAMP

Figure 4-64
Source: http://www.flickr.com © David M. Goehring

Figure 4-65
Source: http://www.flickr.com © momentcaptured1

Figure 4-66
Source: http://www.flickr.com © JAGwired

Figure 4-67
Source: http://www.flickr.com © Jeremy Levine Design

Figure 4-70
Source: http://www.flickr.com © Mat Tyrrell

Figure 4-71
Source: http://www.flickr.com © Jeremy Levine Design

Figure 4-72
Source: http://www.flickr.com © JAGwired

Figure 4-73
Source: http://www.flickr.com © Jeremy Levine Design

Figure 4-74
Source: http://www.flickr.com © JAGwired

Figure 4-75
Source: http://www.flickr.com © Jeremy Levine Design

Figure 4-76
Source: http://www.flickr.com © Jeremy Levine Design

FURNISHINGS AND ACCESSORIES

Individual pieces of furniture or decoration can also serve as great inspiration. Sometimes focusing on only one particular thing can help to clarify your creative vision, and a single object can be perfect for that.

The bold color but overall simplicity of the dish in Figure 4-83 could be a great basis for a minimalist, retro style website. The flowers and color scheme are decidedly 1970s, but there's a simplicity there, too.

Figure 4-84 offers subtle inspiration in the white chaise. There's the leather texture, the pattern created by the tufting, and the general shape. All could be incorporated into a website quite easily.

The pillow in Figure 4-93 could also make a great basis for a website. There's the fabric texture, the color scheme, and the slightly organic shape of the pillow to draw from, all of which could be adapted to a website design, not to mention the nature motif.

Individual furnishings and accessories are often lacking context, so pay more attention to details in the images here, and how you might incorporate similar elements into your designs.

Figure 4-79
Source: http://www.flickr.com © Jessica F.

Figure 4-82
Source: http://www.flickr.com © sunshinecity

Figure 4-83
Source: http://www.flickr.com © Wendy Piersall

Figure 4-84
Source: http://www.flickr.com © Jason Auch

Figure 4-87
Source: http://www.flickr.com © Horia Varlan

Figure 4-90
Source: http://www.flickr.com © cuttlefish / Lauren

Figure 4-91
Source: http://www.flickr.com © ilovebutter

Figure 4-94
Source: http://www.flickr.com © Jenni Douglas

PRODUCT DESIGN

Products surround us, everywhere we look. And there's a wealth of possible design inspiration in even the most basic of objects. Everything from toys to pens to cameras can give you ideas for website designs, if you only take the time to really look at them.

The amount of time and effort that goes into the most basic of product designs often far exceeds the time spent on developing even complex websites. There are decades of research on designing products that doesn't yet exist in the online design and development sphere, including information applied to usability and consumer appeal. All of those same principles can be applied to web design with a little effort.

TOYS

Children's toys can provide enough inspiration to last a designer a lifetime. Use an action figure for the basis of a color scheme, or a board game as the inspiration for a layout. Virtually any kids' toy can be adapted, at least in part, into a design for a website. Look to this area especially for designs that are meant to be casual, upbeat, or aimed specifically at children.

The toy soldiers in Figure 4-95 could be the basis for a color scheme, while the fake grass on their bases could be used as a texture in a site design. Look, too, to the flourishes and embellishment details included, and think of ways those could be adapted.

The train and tracks in Figure 4-100 have a great, subtle color scheme (shades of gray, mostly, but with that wonderful bright blue, too). There are also some fantastic curves among the tracks, and a general distressed texture to the whole setup that could be applied to a grunge site design.

The aged patina and wear of the toy airplane in Figure 4-106 could also be used as the basis for a grunge site. But the bright red, white, gray, and black color scheme would also be well suited for adoption in a variety of website designs.

Toys often evoke nostalgia in adults, so pay close attention to the mood the images here convey when gathering ideas for your work.

Figure 4-95
Source: http://www.flickr.com © Glen Edelson

Figure 4-97
Source: http://www.flickr.com © Steven Depolo

Figure 4-96
Source: http://www.flickr.com © Horia Varlan

Figure 4-98
Source: http://www.flickr.com © Horia Varlan

Figure 4-99
Source: http://www.flickr.com © Kenny Louie

Figure 4-101
Source: http://www.flickr.com © Nathan Bittinger

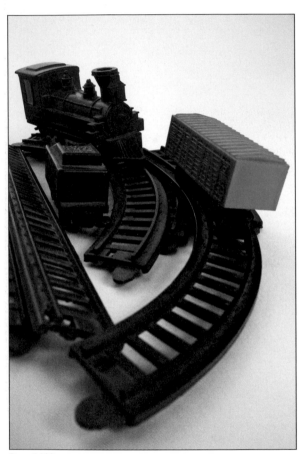

Figure 4-100
Source: http://www.flickr.com © Horia Varlan

Figure 4-102
Source: http://www.flickr.com © Haria Varlan

Figure 4-103
Source: http://www.flickr.com © puuikibeach / davidd

Figure 4-104
Source: http://www.flickr.com © puuikibeach / davidd

Figure 4-105
Source: http://www.flickr.com © puuikibeach / davidd

Figure 4-106
Source: http://www.flickr.com © Dennis Wong

Figure 4-107
Source: http://www.flickr.com © Orin Zebest

Figure 4-108
Source: http://www.flickr.com © Lara604

EVERYDAY ITEMS

The items you use everyday are often overlooked as sources of inspiration, and yet time and effort goes into designing those items. From the pens on your desk to your sunglasses, and everything else around you, there are a host of textures, patterns, shapes, colors, and other design elements you can pull from.

Take the leather journal in Figure 4-111. There are textures in the leather (both the exterior and the bit of interior visible on the bottom). There are also patterns on the cover that could be adapted. The colors are rich and would make an absolutely breathtaking color scheme. Overall, this journal could be turned into fantastic websites well suited to a variety of purposes.

By contrast, look at the simplicity of the pencil lead (graphite) in Figure 4-114. At first glance, it's simple and doesn't seem particularly inspiring. But look closer and you'll see there are stone and wood-grain textures there, as well as the beginnings of a great color scheme. It's all a matter of adjusting the way you look at the world.

Even something as common as an old pair of shoes, like those in Figure 4-116, could be adapted into a beautiful website. There's the leather texture, as well as the fabric texture of the shoelaces and the brass eyeholes. In addition, there's a subtle color scheme present, and some great organic shapes.

Everyday items can sometimes present clever solutions to common problems, so be sure to consider not only the design details in the images in this section, but also what their purpose is and if they've done anything clever with their intended function.

Figure 4-111
Source: http://www.flickr.com © a little tune

Figure 4-112
Source: http://www.flickr.com © puuikibeach / davidd

Figure 4-113
Source: http://www.flickr.com © sebilden / David J

Figure 4-114
Source: http://www.flickr.com © Chris Dlugosz

Figure 4-115
Source: http://www.flickr.com © LWY

Figure 4-116
Source: http://www.flickr.com © Scott Feldstein

Figure 4-117
Source: http://www.flickr.com © bangli 1

Figure 4-118
Source: http://www.flickr.com © theogeo / Lindsey T

Figure 4-119
Source: http://www.flickr.com © Erin O'Connor

Figure 4-120
Source: http://www.flickr.com © Andres Rueda

Figure 4-122
Source: http://www.flickr.com © Horia Varlan

Figure 4-121
Source: http://www.flickr.com © Bill Bradford

Figure 4-123
Source: http://www.flickr.com © Brenda Gottsabend

Figure 4-125
Source: http://www.flickr.com © Alan Levine

Figure 4-124
Source: http://www.flickr.com © Lara604

Figure 4-126
Source: http://www.flickr.com © MIKI Yoshihito

TECHNOLOGY

Technology, whether old or new, can inspire some great modern-looking websites. But turn to older tech and you could probably find the basis for a retro design, too. Within the technology sphere, there are a plethora of shapes, colors, textures, and patterns available to you. Open up some of that technology, and you get even more possibilities.

As a designer, you probably have a ton of technology just sitting on your desk. Looking at my own desk, there are speakers, a smartphone and dock, two lamps, an ebook reader, a mouse and other computer peripherals, plus my laptop. And that's all just within arm's reach. If I were to look through my entire house, I could more than fill a page listing all the technology there, as could most people.

Figure 4-129, as an example, has at least half a dozen textures, a few patterns, and a lot of possible shapes and colors you could use. The internals of just about any electronic device would present a similar number of things to adapt.

The vintage camera in Figure 4-136 has some great textures that could be adapted to either a modern or retro design. The leather texture of the grips combined with the metal alone could be applied in any number of ways. Plus, there are shapes, patterns, and colors present that would be at home on any website.

Considering both modern and vintage technology presents a wider range of possible ideas than strictly current technology, as demonstrated in the images included in this section. Pay attention not only to the details, but also to the way user interfaces are designed, and the purpose behind each design.

Figure 4-127
Source: http://www.flickr.com © LGEPR

Figure 4-128
Source: http://www.flickr.com © Randy Pertiet

Figure 4-129
Source: http://www.flickr.com © Blake Patterson

Figure 4-130
Source: http://www.flickr.com © Mike Hammerton

Figure 4-131
Source: http://www.flickr.com © JVC America

Figure 4-132
Source: http://www.flickr.com © JVC America

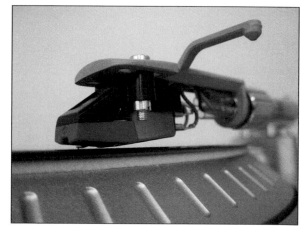

Figure 4-134
Source: http://www.flickr.com © Michelle Hawkins-Thiel

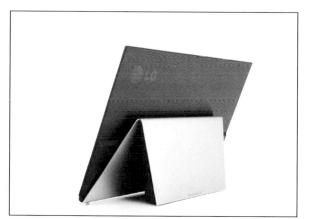

Figure 4-133
Source: http://www.flickr.com © LGEPR

Figure 4-135
Source: http://www.flickr.com © Michael Pereckas

Figure 4-136
Source: http://www.flickr.com © John Nuttall

Figure 4-138
Source: http://www.flickr.com © JVC America

Figure 4-137
Source: http://www.flickr.com © Terren in Virginia

Figure 4-139
Source: http://www.flickr.com © John Loo

Figure 4-140
Source: http://www.flickr.com © Joi Ito

Figure 4-141
Source: http://www.flickr.com © MIKI Yoshihito

Figure 4-142
Source: http://www.flickr.com © MIKI Yoshihito

TEXTILES

Color, texture, and pattern are all prominent elements of textile designs, and can all be adapted at will. Textiles are another extremely common designed area that is usually overlooked when searching for inspiration. But textiles are everywhere, from the clothes you're wearing to the chair you're sitting in to the blankets on your bed.

The fabric in Figure 4-143 could be adapted in a few ways. First, there's the color scheme, which has enough variation that it would be suitable for a website design almost as-is. Then, there's the pattern, which could be used as the basis for a background, or as embellishments to a design. Finally, you have the rather large woven texture of the material, which could also be adapted into a background image.

The blanket in Figure 4-156 also has a few adaptation possibilities. The texture of the blanket is great, as is the plaid pattern. There are plenty of colors to base a color palette on, too.

The fabric in Figure 4-163 is great inspiration, despite its relative simplicity. There are details here, the stitching and slightly glittery appearance mostly, that could be adapted to a website quite easily. Then there's the repeating diamond pattern, and the subtle, monochromatic color scheme, which could also be used effectively.

The textiles images included here are excellent sources of color, texture, and pattern, but can also offer ideas for mood and style.

Figure 4-143
Source: http://www.flickr.com © geishaboy500 / THOR

Figure 4-144
Source: http://www.flickr.com © geishaboy500 / THOR

Figure 4-146
Source: http://www.flickr.com © Andrea Smith

Figure 4-145
Source: http://www.flickr.com © Sherrie Thai

Figure 4-148
Source: http://www.flickr.com © Ged Carroll

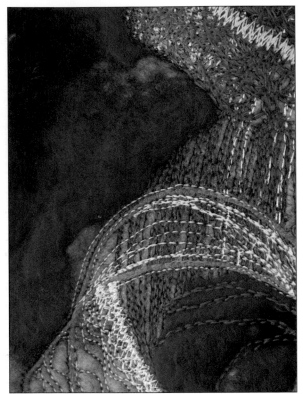

Figure 4-147
Source: http://www.flickr.com © Rachel Reynolds

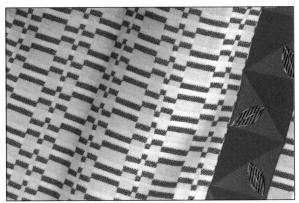

Figure 4-149
Source: http://www.flickr.com © Steve Snodgrass

Figure 4-150
Source: http://www.flickr.com © Sherrie Thai

Figure 4-151
Source: http://www.flickr.com © rajkumar1220

Figure 4-152
Source: http://www.flickr.com © rajkumar1220

Figure 4-153
Source: http://www.flickr.com © Jens Karlsson

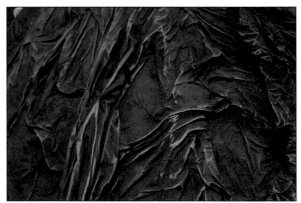

Figure 4-154
Source: http://www.flickr.com © Sherrie Thai

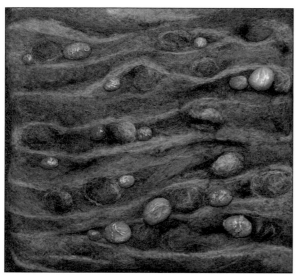

Figure 4-155
Source: http://www.flickr.com © Inger Maaike

Figure 4-157
Source: http://www.flickr.com © Holly Kuchera

Figure 4-156
Source: http://www.flickr.com © lindsay.dee.bunny / Lindsay

Figure 4-158
Source: http://www.flickr.com © Andie712b / Bethany

Figure 4-159
Source: http://www.flickr.com © Rob Walker

Figure 4-161
Source: http://www.flickr.com © Rachel Reynolds

Figure 4-160
Source: http://www.flickr.com © Melanie Tata

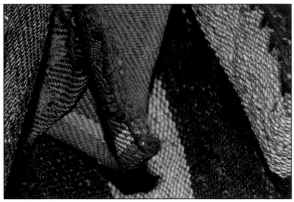

Figure 4-162
Source: http://www.flickr.com © Chris Parfitt

Figure 4-163
Source: http://www.flickr.com © Kit Seaton

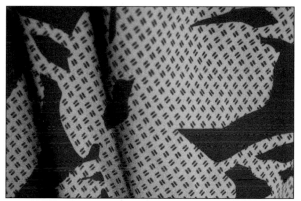

Figure 4-164
Source: http://www.flickr.com © Kit Seaton

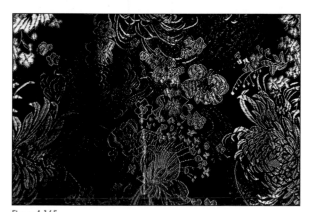

Figure 4-165
Source: http://www.flickr.com © Kit Seaton

Figure 4-166
Source: http://www.flickr.com © Kit Seaton

CONCLUSION

Regardless of where you turn, there are designed objects all around you. As designers, we need to learn to look more closely at those objects, and see the inherent beauty in every example. Even the poorest designs generally have at least one or two lessons you can learn, even if those lessons are what not to do.

PHOTOGRAPHY

5

A CENTURY AGO, photography was something special, something exclusive enjoyed only by the select few who could afford it. There were no portable cameras (at least not in the sense we think of "portable" now), developing photos was a very specialized process, and we were still using plates rather than film.

In the mid-20th century, all of that changed. Cameras became more commonplace. Film was affordable, as was developing said film, and many families had cameras. There was no turning back from there.

Now, just about everyone in the western world has a camera of some sort, often on their smartphone. Photography has become democratized, accessible to just about anyone. The popularity of sites like Flickr only further supports this idea. (Flickr currently hosts well over five billion photos, and it's not even the largest photo-sharing site.)

Considering the ubiquity of the photograph, it would be a shame not to tap into this medium for inspiration for your designs. After all, there are photography styles and subjects to suit just about any design project, and there's a wealth of potential imagery to draw from.

The most obvious way to use a photograph for inspiration is to incorporate the actual image into your design, most commonly done in either a header or the background image. Big backgrounds can create a unique look for an otherwise-minimalist site. But there's a wealth of other possible ideas in many photos, from textures and patterns to color schemes and the ratio of positive to negative space.

BLACK AND WHITE

Black and white (or monochrome) photography was the first type of photography developed. It has come in and out of fashion since then, but is enjoying resurgence with the wealth of smartphone applications that include black and white filters. Many digital cameras also include native support for black and white photos, and it's one of the easiest effects to achieve with photo-editing software.

When looking at black and white photos, there are a number of things you can potentially use for inspiration. Shapes and forms can stand out more in a black and white image, when you're not distracted by colors. Negative and positive space is also more apparent in many black and white images.

In Figure 5-3, for example, very bold shapes are present, created by the interweaving train tracks. There are also some great textures here—gritty asphalt, shiny steel, and diamond plate. It's a relatively simple image, and yet it provides a wealth of possible ideas.

Figure 5-7 also has some very bold forms: wavy lines in this case. There's the weathered woodgrain texture of the bench seat and back, and the concrete ground visible between the slats to pull ideas from, too. The composition of the photo—the way the wavy lines direct attention toward certain parts of the image, specifically *into* the image—shouldn't be overlooked, either.

Figure 5-15 is filled with orderly, geometric shapes. The brick of the buildings could be used as the basis for a pattern. The tower has some great textures, both in the upright supports and in the structure at the top. The negative space of the sky could be emulated in any kind of design. It's also a good example of balance in an asymmetrical image.

The rest of the images in this section are also great examples of black and white photography. Pay attention to the elements already mentioned, but don't be afraid to draw ideas from other aspects.

Figure 5-1
Source: www.flickr.com © Evan Mitchell

Figure 5-2
Source: www.flickr.com © Jamie Henderson

Figure 5-3
Source: www.flickr.com © bachmont

Figure 5-4
Source: www.flickr.com © Alan Turkus

Figure 5-5
Source: www.flickr.com © Kevin Collins

Figure 5-6
Source: www.flickr.com © Jamie Henderson

Figure 5-7
Source: www.flickr.com © Jamie Henderson

Figure 5-8
Source: www.flickr.com © J.W.Photography

Figure 5-10
Source: www.flickr.com © Linda Rae

Figure 5-9
Source: www.flickr.com © Sean McGrath

Figure 5-11
Source: www.flickr.com © Bird Eye

Figure 5-12
Source: www.flickr.com © Alex Proimos

Figure 5-13
Source: www.flickr.com © Frank Kovalchek

Figure 5-14
Source: www.flickr.com © Matthias Rhomberg

Figure 5-15
Source: www.flickr.com © Jen and a Camera

Figure 5-16
Source: www.flickr.com © Kirsty Andrews

Figure 5-17
Source: www.flickr.com © Randen Pederson

Figure 5-18
Source: www.flickr.com © Bruno Postigo

Figure 5-19
Source: www.flickr.com © Perry McKenna

Figure 5-20
Source: www.flickr.com © Steve Snodgrass

EFFECTS

A lot of possible effects can be achieved with photography, either through settings on the camera itself, filters in a camera app, or post-processing in photo-editing software. Some of these effects are designed to mimic the styles of certain kinds of photos or cameras (such as *lomography*), whereas others are designed to create more dynamic or interesting images.

Color is one of the most obvious things to draw inspiration from in special effects photography. Many effects have a direct impact on the colors present in the image, whether those colors are brighter and more saturated (like in HDR and Velvia images) or shifted from the originals (like in lomography photos).

Other things to look at include textures—especially textures in the background of an image—lighting, negative space, and perspective.

HDR

HDR, or High Dynamic Range, photos are characterized by brighter, more saturated colors and more contrast than traditional photos. There are two kinds of HDR, and sometimes it can be difficult to tell the difference between the two. The first kind is a true HDR photo, which is actually a composite of multiple photos taken at different exposures. The second type is simulated HDR, and is created by adjusting the shadows and highlights in an image with a program like Adobe Photoshop.

It's possible for both techniques to be combined to create an even more stunning image. Regardless of the method used to achieve the final image, HDR photos can be a great source of color schemes and textures.

Figure 5-21 offers a couple of strong ideas that could be translated for design projects. The dark, brooding mood of the storm clouds is probably the most obvious idea. The color scheme here is usable, too, with the shades of dark gray interspersed with highlights of orange and gold.

Figure 5-28 offers some great shapes and textures to work with. There are lots of vertical and diagonal lines that could be used. Rust textures are also present, and there are some great colors you could build a color scheme around.

Figure 5-36 also has some amazing colors: the blue-green of the ocean, the blue of the sky, the off-white in the cliffs, and the oranges and greens of the foliage and ground. There's a striped pattern in the cliff face, as well as stone textures.

The other photos here are also great examples of HDR technique. Look at color and mood, but consider other elements in each image, too, such as texture or composition.

Figure 5-21
Source: www.flickr.com © Geoff Sloan

Figure 5-22
Source: www.flickr.com © Randy Pertiet

Figure 5-23
Source: www.flickr.com © Randy Pertiet

Figure 5-24
Source: www.flickr.com © Jamie Henderson

Figure 5-25
Source: www.flickr.com © Ricardo Hurtubia

Figure 5-26
Source: www.flickr.com © kdinuraj / Dinuraj K

Figure 5-27
Source: www.flickr.com © Neil Henderson

Figure 5-28
Source: www.flickr.com © Tim Fields

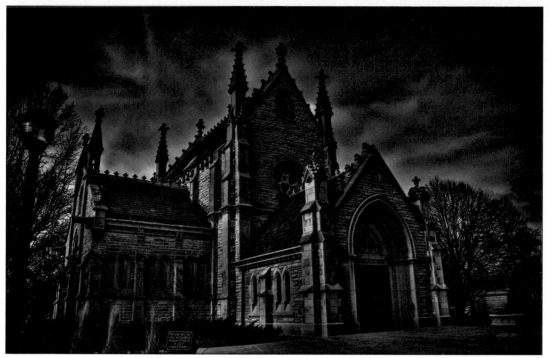

Figure 5-29
Source: www.flickr.com © Paul J Everett

Figure 5-30
Source: www.flickr.com © Russ Bowling

Figure 5-31
Source: www.flickr.com © phylevn

Figure 5-32
Source: www.flickr.com © Paul Tomlin

Figure 5-33
Source: www.flickr.com © Robert Lowe

Figure 5-34
Source: www.flickr.com © Juan Carlos Labbe

Figure 5-35
Source: www.flickr.com © Randy Pertiet

Figure 5-36
Source: www.flickr.com © Vincent Joly

Figure 5-37
Source: www.flickr.com © David J Laporte

Figure 5-38
Source: www.flickr.com © Mohammed Al-Naser

Figure 5-39
Source: www.flickr.com © David DeHetre

Figure 5-40
Source: www.flickr.com © Patrick Malone

LOMOGRAPHY

Lomography was originally created using cameras manufactured in the USSR in the 1980s. The cameras were of relatively poor quality, and often had issues with light leaking into the camera body, which resulted in odd exposures. But people found the unpredictable nature of images taken with LOMO cameras to be endearing, and the cameras developed quite a following. Photos taken with LOMO cameras are also often cross-processed, resulting in strange color effects. Double-exposed photos are sometimes seen, too.

Lomography is sometimes used to describe almost any kind of low-quality, "leaky" (the term used when light leaks into the camera body) photograph, even though only photos taken on a true LOMO camera are technically lomographs. Many smartphone camera apps include lomography and similar filters, and lomography effects can be achieved in photo-editing programs.

Look for color schemes, textures, and even grunge effects in LOMO photos. Figure 5-42 has various shades of red and orange set against a blue background, which could serve as the basis for a color scheme. The image is slightly out of focus and has strong vignetting that could be emulated in a design, too.

The color scheme in Figure 5-46, the purple and orange especially, could be adapted to a design. The soft lighting effects could also be duplicated. Beyond that, there's the shape and texture of the stone or concrete structure in the foreground that could be adapted for a design.

The daisies in Figure 5-58 could be used as a motif in a design, either literally or abstractly. There's a strong color scheme here of orange, white, and green, too. The photo has strong vignetting and a dark mood considering the usually cheerful subject.

The other lomographs in this section have elements similar to those already mentioned, but with their own unique take.

Figure 5-41
Source: www.flickr.com © Bolshakov

Figure 5-42
Source: www.flickr.com © cliffchen1973

Figure 5-45
Source: www.flickr.com © Christian H.

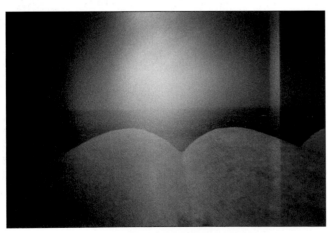

Figure 5-46
Source: www.flickr.com © Christian H.

Figure 5-47
Source: www.flickr.com © Michael Warren

Figure 5-50
Source: www.flickr.com © Kevin Dooley

Figure 5-48
Source: www.flickr.com © Anthony Majanlahti

Figure 5-51
Source: www.flickr.com © Kevin Dooley

Figure 5-49
Source: www.flickr.com © John.Purvis

Figure 5-52
Source: www.flickr.com © judepics / Judith

Figure 5-53
Source: www.flickr.com © Cameron Russell

Figure 5-54
Source: www.flickr.com © Michael Warren

Figure 5-55
Source: www.flickr.com © Michael Warren

Figure 5-56
Source: www.flickr.com © Michael Warren

Figure 5-57
Source: www.flickr.com © Michael Warren

Figure 5-58
Source: www.flickr.com © Michael Warren

Figure 5-59
Source: www.flickr.com © Christian H.

Figure 5-60
Source: www.flickr.com © Christian H.

OTHER EFFECTS

There are dozens, if not hundreds, of effects that can be achieved with a camera and photo-editing software. Smartphone apps often have dozens of filters that can be applied to an image. Post-processing of photos can achieve more effects, or enhance the ones created by the camera app.

Tilt shift images, for example, use blurring techniques (or special lenses) to create photos of landscapes or people that make the subjects look miniaturized, or like toys. Selective color creates a mostly black and white image with one or two bright bursts of color. Velvia film was known for producing very bright, saturated photos and became popular with nature photographers because of this. There are also photos taken with pinhole cameras, infrared cameras, and with soft focus filters.

Figure 5-65 has a definite grunge look. Both the border and the graininess of the image could be used in a design. Beyond that, there's plenty there to serve as the basis of a color scheme, especially the bright bursts of pink in the flowers.

Figure 5-69 is a tilt-shift photo. It has a somewhat-magical, fantastic mood and style, caused by the snow and the miniature look of the bridge. That mood is perfect for adaptation.

Figure 5-77 is filled with great texture ideas. There's the bark and moss in the background, as well as the underside of the mushrooms. The blurry, dark nature of the image offers ideas for the mood and tone of a design.

The other effects applied to the photos here offer a wealth of ideas spanning virtually every possible design element, from composition to color palettes to mood.

Figure 5-61
Source: www.flickr.com © Brad Gillette

Figure 5-62
Source: www.flickr.com © Aaron Alexander

Figure 5-63
Source: www.flickr.com © Aaron Alexander

Figure 5-65
Source: www.flickr.com © Brad Gillette

Figure 5-64
Source: www.flickr.com © Aaron Alexander

Figure 5-66
Source: www.flickr.com © Brad Gillette

Figure 5-67
Source: www.flickr.com © Paolo Camera

Figure 5-68
Source: www.flickr.com © Eduardo Millo

Figure 5-69
Source: www.flickr.com © Listener42 / Josh

Figure 5-70
Source: www.flickr.com © Lars Christopher Nøttaasen

Figure 5-71
Source: www.flickr.com © Neff Conner

Figure 5-72
Source: www.flickr.com © ryPix / Ryan

Figure 5-73
Source: www.flickr.com © Stewart Chambers

Figure 5-74
Source: www.flickr.com © Luis Argerich

Figure 5-75
Source: www.flickr.com © Luis Argerich

Figure 5-77
Source: www.flickr.com © Hans Pama

Figure 5-76
Source: www.flickr.com © Cody Long

Figure 5-78
Source: www.flickr.com © Harry Nguyen

Figure 5-79
Source: www.flickr.com © Sung Ming Whang

Figure 5-80
Source: www.flickr.com © Stewart Butterfield

CLASSIC PHOTOGRAPHY

While artistic and stylized photography can offer a lot of inspiration, so can "regular" photography—the kind you might find everywhere from a family photo album to a professional photo studio. Until recently, this type of photography was the most commonly seen, and would likely still be the only type of photos most people would see if it weren't for the popularity of apps that make special effects easy for the everyday user.

Classic photography generally focuses on one of three general categories: people, landscapes, and macros (extreme close-ups). All three types of photos can be taken with anything from a basic digital camera or smartphone camera to a more advanced DSLR.

The main thing that stands out among classic photography is that composition is often the most important part of a "great" photograph. Where photos with special effects can hide behind those effects to look more stylish, classic photos without overt effects have to stand on the merit of the composition—including the interaction of the background and foreground and the balance of the image—and subject of the photo itself. Pay careful attention to the composition of the images in this section, in addition to the colors, textures, and other elements.

PEOPLE

Whether portraits or group photos, posed or spontaneous, photographs of people can hold a wealth of possible ideas. There are textures, shadows and highlights, colors, patterns, mood, and more in many of these images.

Photos of people have a long history. Portraits were some of the most popular early photographs, and having "your picture made" was a special occasion. Photos of people have grown more spontaneous over the years, at least in part because of advances in photo technology.

In Figure 5-86 there are a number of textures that could be used: snow, fur hat and vest, and leather gloves. There's also the color scheme: blue, white (and off-white), black, and shades of brown. The way the branches are in front of the face lends depth to the image and helps the viewer's eye focus on the face. It makes it feel as if you're in the forest, not just looking at an image. And don't forget the somewhat-fantastical mood of the image.

Figure 5-94 could be translated almost directly into a layout. The blue and white pattern on the top could be the basis of a header. The baby and trim in the background could be the basis for the main content area. And the wood grain at the bottom could be a footer. Photos rarely present ideas that could be translated this directly, but it does happen sometimes and is something worth looking for.

Figure 5-99 is a more abstract portrait, with the reflection of a person the subject, rather than the actual person. The use of negative space here offers some ideas, as does the texture of the concrete. Don't overlook the reflective quality of the water, which is suited for adaptation.

The other photos of people in this section can provide ideas for mood, texture, composition, and other elements already mentioned. The people are only one aspect of the image to look at; make sure you're also paying attention to background, negative space, and other secondary elements.

Figure 5-81
Source: www.dreamstime.com © Starletdarlene

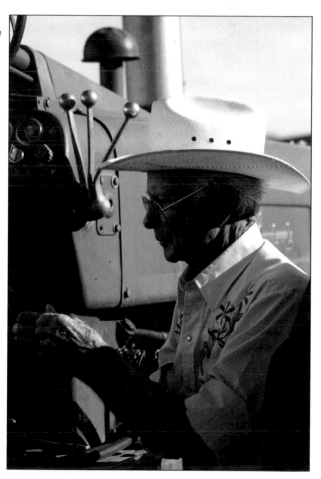

Figure 5-84
Source: www.flickr.com © Stig Nygaard

Figure 5-85
Source: www.flickr.com © Robb North

Figure 5-86
Source: www.dreamstime.com © Alexander Smirnov

Figure 5-87
Source: www.flickr.com © Gilberto Santa Rosa

Figure 5-88
Source: www.flickr.com © Zach Dischner

Figure 5-89
Source: www.dreamstime.com © Almaterra

Figure 5-90
Source: www.flickr.com © Anthony Kelly

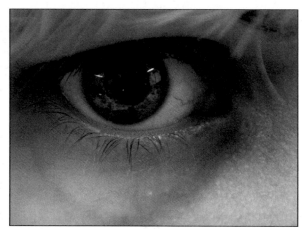

Figure 5-91
Source: www.flickr.com © Deborah Austin

Figure 5-92
Source: www.flickr.com © Jeff Turner

Figure 5-93
Source: www.flickr.com © Karri Huhtanen

Figure 5-94
Source: www.dreamstime.com © Crystal Kirk

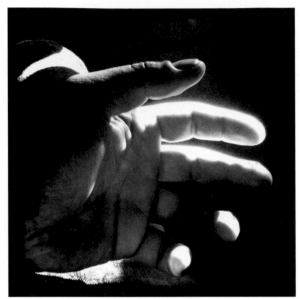

Figure 5-95
Source: www.flickr.com © Michele Africano

Figure 5-97
Source: www.dreamstime.com © Stanislav Perov

Figure 5-96
Source: www.flickr.com © John Steven Fernandez

Figure 5-98
Source: www.flickr.com © Paul Hart

LANDSCAPES

Landscapes also have a long history in the world of photography. Virtually everyone with a camera takes a landscape photo at one point or another, and some of the most recognizable photos ever taken are landscapes (just think of the photos Ansel Adams took during the Great Depression for evidence of this).

Like other photos, landscapes provide a wealth of color and texture ideas, as well as ideas for composition, the ratio of negative space, patterns, and mood. Whether the subject is a traditional mountain scene, a waterscape, a cityscape, or something else entirely, landscapes are easy to find and accessible to anyone.

Figure 5-102 has an ominous mood, created by the foggy landscape and dark colors. The winding river gives a sense of movement, though. One of the best ideas you might get from this photo, though, is the sense of multiple layers created by the fog partially obscuring some of the mountains. This layered effect is perfect for many design projects.

The colors in Figure 5-111 could be the basis for a beautiful color scheme. The blues of the lake and the greens of the hills are the most striking colors present, but there are also shades of gray and brown present throughout.

Figure 5-117 is filled with textures: rocks, foliage, and dirt primarily. The brown and muted green colors in the image could be turned into a color palette for a design without much modification.

The remaining photos here are more great examples of landscapes that can influence every element of your designs.

Figure 5-101
Source: www.flickr.com © Peter Rivera

Figure 5-102
Source: www.flickr.com © Nishanth Jois

Figure 5-103
Source: www.flickr.com © Edwart Visser

Figure 5-104
Source: www.flickr.com © NeilsPhotography

Figure 5-105
Source: www.flickr.com © ben124. / Berit

Figure 5-106
Source: www.flickr.com © ben124. / Berit

Figure 5-107
Source: www.flickr.com © Börkur Sigurbjörnsson

Figure 5-108
Source: www.flickr.com © epcp

Figure 5-109
Source: www.flickr.com © davidgsteadman

Figure 5-110
Source: www.flickr.com © Roy Lathwell

Figure 5-111
Source: www.flickr.com © Frank Kovalchek

Figure 5-112
Source: www.flickr.com © McKay Savage

Figure 5-113
Source: www.flickr.com © Frank Kovalchek

Figure 5-114
Source: www.flickr.com © Billy Lindblom

Figure 5-115
Source: www.flickr.com © Christian Guthier

Figure 5-116
Source: www.flickr.com © Ian Carroll

Figure 5-117
Source: www.flickr.com © Bryce Edwards

Figure 5-118
Source: www.flickr.com © NeilsPhotography

Figure 5-119
Source: www.flickr.com © Roy Lathwell

Figure 5-120
Source: www.flickr.com © Richard Gould

MACRO

Macro photos (sometimes mistakenly called "micro" photos) are extreme close-ups. Popular subjects include insects, flowers and plants, electronics, and other small objects. Macros can give an entirely new perspective on a subject.

Textures are generally made much more apparent in macro photos. Patterns, if they exist in the subject, are also amplified. And of course you can get ideas from the shapes, colors, and mood of a macro photo, like any other photo.

Figure 5-123 is a close-up of what looks like a flower bud. There's an obvious pattern present (the overlapping petals), as well as a great texture (the speckled surface of the petals). The colors present could be turned into a beautiful, soft color palette that would be perfectly suited to a feminine design.

Figure 5-125 is a monarch butterfly that looks fully formed, but is still inside its cocoon. The colors here, especially the iridescent surface of the cocoon, are stunning, and offer a wealth of possible ideas. Other ideas can be drawn from the texture of the cocoon's surface and the wall it's attached to, and the bold black lines visible in the butterfly's wings.

Figure 5-127 is a close-up of a frog's eye. The shimmering surface of the eye's iris, as well as the frog's skin, is the most prominent feature of the photo. There are also the colors present: the copper of the eye and the green of the frog's skin. Either could be the basis of a color scheme (or, they could be combined in a bolder design).

The other macro photos in this section include a host of other ideas for your designs, and can be especially helpful in coming up with details that will set your designs apart.

Figure 5-121
Source: www.flickr.com © Lisa Cee

Figure 5-122
Source: www.flickr.com © yellowcloud

Figure 5-123
Source: www.flickr.com © mythlady

Figure 5-124
Source: www.flickr.com © Shiny Things

Figure 5-125
Source: www.flickr.com © puuikibeach / davidd

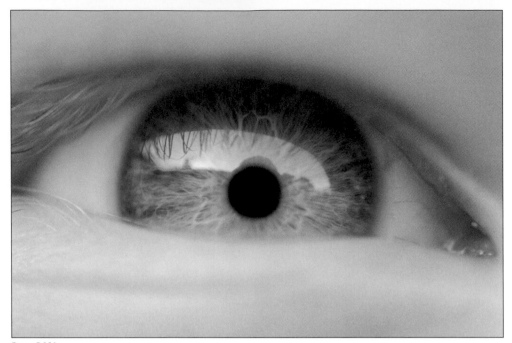

Figure 5-126
Source: www.flickr.com © Steve Lodefink

Figure 5-127
Source: www.flickr.com © August Kelm

Figure 5-128
Source: www.flickr.com © Horia Varlan

Figure 5-129
Source: www.flickr.com © Maschinenraum

Figure 5-130
Source: www.flickr.com © Noel Feans

Figure 5-131
Source: www.flickr.com © Chris Dlugosz

Figure 5-132
Source: www.flickr.com © Chris Dlugosz

Figure 5-133
Source: www.flickr.com © Lara604

Figure 5-134
Source: www.flickr.com © Orin Zebest

Figure 5-135
Source: www.flickr.com © backpackphotography / B D

Figure 5-136
Source: www.flickr.com © Jared Tarbell

Figure 5-137
Source: www.flickr.com © Jameel Winter

Figure 5-138

Source: www.flickr.com © Scott Robinson

Figure 5-139
Source: www.flickr.com © pasukaru76 / Pascal

Figure 5-140
Source: www.flickr.com © Emran Kassim

CONCLUSION

Photography may be the most accessible form of art out there. Virtually everyone in the developed world (not to mention a large part of the developing world) has access to a camera, whether it's a feature of a cell phone or a stand-alone gadget. Photography has invaded our lives online, with photo sharing and social networking sites serving as primary points for photo distribution from our friends, family, and colleagues. The work of photographers, both amateur and professional, can be called up online in just a few seconds.

With such a wealth of potential ideas at our fingertips, it only makes sense that designers would learn to utilize this vast resource. Learning to pick and choose elements from something as organic as many photographs is a valuable skill that can serve designers whenever they're lacking inspiration.

USING

INSPIRATION

CREATING SOMETHING NEW FROM DIRECT INSPIRATION 6

DIRECT INSPIRATION IS often easier to get ideas from than more abstract sources. Looking at other web designs can lead directly to new ideas and new ways to use existing ones. But it's also very easy to draw a bit too much from a single source and inadvertently copy someone else's design. That's why it's important to be methodical in how you use inspiration from direct sources, to make sure you're not infringing on someone else's intellectual property.

DISSECTING A DESIGN

Hopefully, by the time you get to this point, you'll already have some designs in mind that you love. Some of these will be similar to the project you're about to tackle, whereas others will be wildly different, either in tone, content, or style (or all three). The first thing you'll need to do is take a close look at the designs you'd like to pull ideas from.

For this chapter, you're going to create a blog design, for a personal blog. This is going to be for a fun, modern personal blog, aimed at hip 20-somethings. Virtually every designer out there is going to be called upon to create a blog design at some point or other (unless they specifically don't do blog design), so it's close to common ground.

Let's start with the top-level elements like mood, layout, and color scheme. Once you have these things down, it's easier to start choosing the more specific elements you want to adapt.

For the mood, you're going to look at the site for the Munch 5-a-Day iPhone app shown in Figure 6-1. It has a light, positive mood, created by the delicate color scheme, light use of typography, and plenty of space around design elements. There's nothing dark or brooding here.

How Do You Choose Designs?

The answer to this question is fairly simple: Pick designs you like. It doesn't matter why you like them, only that you do. There are almost always elements to pull ideas from in any good design. The same goes for picking individual elements from the designs you like: choose the parts you like best. It can help to make a list of the elements you need (header, footer, layout, colors, typography, and so on), and then go through the sites picking and choosing the best of each.

Figure 6-1: Inspiration for the site's mood.
Source: www.munch5aday.com © MeYou Health, LLC

Next, look at the layout. Now, since layout is often one of the most recognizable elements of a design, you're going to take inspiration for the layout from two different websites. This helps prevent any inadvertent copying. For the basic layout, let's use the Elegant Seagulls site, shown in Figure 6-2.

Figure 6-2: Inspiration for the site's general layout.
Source: www.elegantseagulls.com © Elegant Seagulls

Note the geometric background and simple main content area.

For the layout inside the main content area, let's draw inspiration from the two-column design used by Hoban Press, as shown in Figure 6-3.

Figure 6-3: More layout inspiration.
Source: www.hobancards.com © Hoban Press

The color scheme will be adapted from Sven Curth's website, which has a really bold blue, lime green, and cream-colored color scheme, as shown in Figure 6-4. It's a fun and modern color scheme, which ties into the mood and tone of this site perfectly.

So now you have the main, top-level elements picked out. There are some great elements to work with there. The main goal when you move on to the design stage is to use these elements as the inspiration for the design, without copying any of them outright. If someone looked at the two sites side-by-side, they might be able to see the relationship, but not in any meaningful way.

Let's move on to some more specific elements. The header and footer of a site are both important elements—like the bookends of any good design. The header on the Coco Suites site, shown in Figure 6-5, is simple but eye-catching, with navigation and branding combined.

Figure 6-4: Color scheme inspiration.
Source: www.svencurth.com © Sven Curth. Designed by Jim Gunardson

Figure 6-5: Inspiration for the site's header.
Source: www.cocosuites.com © Coco Suites

The footer of the Nordic Ruby conference, shown in Figure 6-6, includes some basic information about the conference, a few links, and a logo. It's simple and understated, and perfectly integrated into the rest of the design.

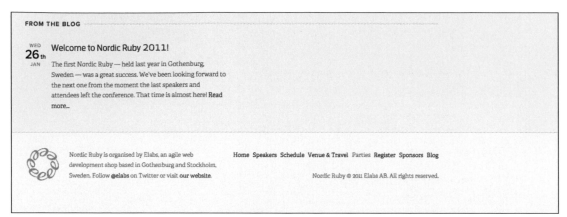

Figure 6-6: Footer inspiration.
Source: www.nordicruby.org © Elabs AB

You now have all the most basic elements of a design: header, footer, layout, color scheme, and mood. You're still missing two major design elements, though: the typography for the site, and some details. Great designs generally have details that set them apart from "good" designs. The details of a site can be pulled from virtually anywhere.

For the typography of this sample site, let's use the Eight Hour Day site as a basis (see Figure 6-7). Consider only the most basic elements, though: a capitalized, sans serif typeface for most the headlines on the site; a traditional serif typeface for the body text; and a script for an accent or two.

Figure 6-7: Inspiration for typography for the site.
Source: eighthourday.com © Eight Hour Day

Let's start with the repeating dot motif from the Every Guyed website, shown in Figure 6-8. There are dots and dotted lines used in numerous places in their design.

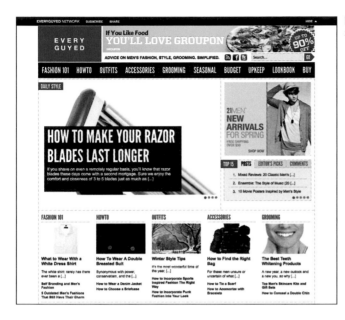

Figure 6-8: Detail inspiration.
Source: www.everyguyed.com © Every Guyed

And let's take a look at the textures used in the Amazee Labs site, shown in Figure 6-9. The grunge texture in the background of this site is a common element, and might be a bit unexpected in a site with a light and airy mood like the one you're designing in this chapter.

Figure 6-9: More detail inspiration.
Source: www.amazeelabs.com © Amazee Labs

Now you have all of the elements, but if you just combined them as they are, you'd have no coherence to the site. It would just be a bunch of random elements, with easily identifiable sources. So you need to adapt these elements to fit your goals and purpose.

ADAPTING INDIVIDUAL ELEMENTS

Let's start with a basic mockup of a design, like you would with any website design, whether it's based on ideas from other sites or not.

The color scheme will come first, although you can change it a bit as you go to fit the elements you have. Based on the Sven Curth design earlier in the chapter, you might come up with a color scheme that looks like the one shown in Figure 6-10 (the green and cream colors are identical to those used in the original design, whereas the blues are shifted a bit more toward the green end of the spectrum).

Figure 6-10: The final color scheme.

Recall that you'll use the basic layout of the Elegant Seagulls design: a simple content area and a geometric background. The geometric background should not be too similar to the original (remember, you want ideas, not copyright infringement), so you could try a nice tartan pattern, as shown in Figure 6-11.

You've already started putting the color scheme in place. The content area is going to use the cream color (#F6F8EF), while the tartan uses the medium blue (#447876). By giving the design a lighter background, you're adapting the color scheme from the original site to fit your own needs.

Immediately following this, I added in some of the dot and texture details from the idea sites. Some designers may opt to add these details last, after they have all the basic design elements in position, which is fine, too. Whether you're building a site based on others or not, your design process should remain whatever works best for you.

Dotted lines are now in place to delineate the header area and the footer, as shown in Figure 6-12. More dotted lines will be added later, as the content fills in. The main content area also now has a very subtle grunge texture that's reminiscent of the one used by Amazee Labs throughout its website.

Figure 6-11: The initial background.

Figure 6-12: Adding some details inspired by the Every Guyed site.

You'll notice in the header design that I've moved the space for the logo to the right side of the design, rather than the left. This is one of the ways you could make it look different than the Coco Suites site, which is where the basic idea came from.

Since you're about to start setting the type, it's time to choose the typefaces. Recall that you need a modern, geometric sans serif face; a traditional serif; and a nice script. For this design, you could try these three fonts that are all freely available through Google Web Fonts: Josefin Sans by Santiago Orozco for the sans serif, Goudy Bookletter 1911 by Barry Schwartz for the serif, and Dancing Script by Pablo Impallari for the script. All three fonts are very legible, which is very important in a text-heavy blog design, as shown in Figure 6-13.

Using different typefaces that have the same style as the original inspiration keeps the new design unique.

Let's put the logo, navigation, and filler text into the header and see how it looks, as shown in Figure 6-14.

Use Dancing Script for the filler text (which on the live site might include a quote, a tagline, or similar short text), and the Josefin Sans for the navigation and site name (it's also used in the logo). You'll notice that there's no serif type yet; you can save it for the body text.

Josefin Sans
Goudy Bookletter 1911
Dancing Script

Figure 6-13: The typeface combination being used.

Figure 6-14: The initial header design.

For the text here, let's use the two shades of blue from the color scheme. These are highly readable against the cream-colored background.

If you compare the header of the design with the Coco Suites header, as shown in Figure 6-15, you'll see that the two are slightly similar, but not at all likely to be confused with one another.

Figure 6-15: The site header compared to the inspiration source.
Coco Suites Source: www.cocosuites.com © Coco Suites

The main content of the design is going to be based on the two-column layout from the Hoban Cards website. Since this is a blog design, you'll need to add some text under each image. Again, because layout is so easily recognizable, it's important to take care to make your layout unique from your inspiration. Adding details and extra content (or removing content and details in the original) is just one way to achieve this. See Figure 6-16.

Figure 6-16: The layout, based on the Hoban Press site.

Note at this point, too, that I've added some more dotted lines between the article headers and excerpts. If you're like me and you don't wait until the end to add all your details, you may want to review at various stages along the way to see where additional detail can improve your design. To keep everything coherent, almost all of the dots used in the design (including the big dot in the logo, but not including the dots in the navigation) are the same lime green color.

Now you can move on to the footer. The inspiration for the footer has more to do with content than the design itself. The Nordic Ruby Conference includes a brief "about" area in its footer, along with navigation and copyright information, as shown in Figure 6-17. This is a fairly common footer design, and isn't generally recognizable from one site to the next.

If you compare that footer to the inspiration site, you'll see that it's similar (see Figure 6-18), but the various elements included in the new design set it apart enough that it's unlikely to be accused of being copied.

Figure 6-17: Detail of the footer.

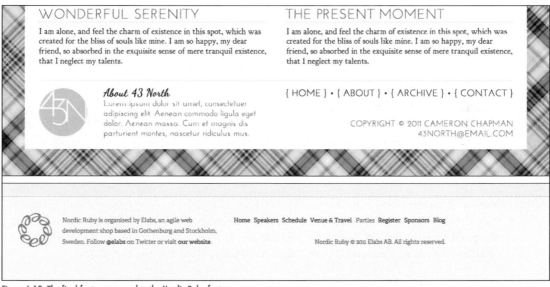

Figure 6-18: The final footer compared to the Nordic Ruby footer.
Nordic Ruby Conference Source: www.nordicruby.org © Elabs AB

Figure 6-19 shows the final design, based on all of the sites of inspiration.

Figure 6-19: The final design.

Pretty hard to recognize any one element as being from a specific site, right? This is the end goal of drawing inspiration from other sites: to create something that is uniquely yours.

CONCLUSION

One of the keys to designing based on other sites is to pull from as many sources as you can. When you draw inspiration from multiple elements on only one or two sites, it's usually easy to pick out exactly where the design comes from. No designer wants to see her work blatantly copied, just like no designer wants to be labeled a thief.

By drawing from eight, nine, ten, or more sources, your end design is unlikely to be similar enough to any one source of ideas to constitute copyright infringement or intellectual property theft. In fact, with some practice, most people (designers included) would never be able to pinpoint where you got your inspiration.

CREATING SOMETHING NEW FROM ABSTRACT INSPIRATION

7

THE PREVIOUS CHAPTER covered how to take elements from existing website designs and adapt them for your own purposes. It's a fairly straightforward process, and one that's easy to emulate for almost any project.

Now, let's move on to creating a design from an abstract source of ideas. These abstract sources might include non-web designs (including architecture or interior design), photos, or your general surroundings.

One advantage to creating sites based on abstract sources is that it's nearly impossible to copy an existing design in a recognizable form. You can create a site based entirely on a single image and many people would be hard-pressed to identify your source of inspiration, even when comparing the two side-by-side. This makes abstract inspiration less risky, from both an ethical and a legal standpoint.

DISSECTING AN IMAGE

You'll start by figuring out how to dissect an image to see what elements you might be able to use in a design. To do this, you're going to look at the actual images from which you'll create an original design. I discuss things in terms of images, because even if you're basing your design on, say, the design of a building, you'll likely be looking at an image of the building in question.

For this project, you're going to design a site for a fictional paranormal romance author, Ramona Black. The site needs to appeal to women, especially women in their 20s and 30s. It also needs to have a simple design, but not minimalist (in keeping with genre and industry conventions), and it needs to look professional.

Start with mood. The mood of your website can have a huge impact on the other elements, so it's important to figure that out early on.

Figure 7-1 is grungy, but it's also bright and positive feeling, which is uncommon for a grungy image. Since paranormal romance tends to be grittier than other romance sub-genres, this kind of mood works well.

Next, you can find some inspiration for the color scheme. Popular colors for paranormal romance are generally reds and purples, so it's a good idea to stick to that general theme, but maybe see if you can give it a twist. Sticking close to the "norm" for this kind of site makes it more easily recognizable to the author's target readership. Think about the kinds of objects that generally include those colors for an idea of where to start looking. Flowers come most immediately to mind. Figure 7-2 has some great shades of purple, plus it has some nice gray shades in the background that you could use. Gray isn't as often seen on this kind of website, so it's one way to set this site apart from its competition.

Figure 7-1: Grungy, but bright and upbeat feeling.
Source: Flickr.com © Karl-Ludwig Poggemann

Figure 7-2: Flowers and other natural objects can be great sources of ideas for color schemes.
Source: Flickr.com © Tom Bech

Since Ramona Black's books take place in natural areas, like the forest, you could look for an image along those lines to use in the header. Incorporating an image directly into a design is one of the simplest ideas, but can also be quite powerful if it's the right image. Figure 7-3 is just the right kind of image. The path leading off into the woods has the right kind of feel for the site, and the main focus of the image takes place along a rather narrow horizontal section of the photo, which makes it great for a header.

You're also going to need some kind of idea for your page layout. This can be one of the hardest things to find among abstract inspiration. Turning to something like a book layout or other design can work, and that's what you'll do here. Figure 7-4 shows a page from an old book, with an interesting layout that switches between a single column and a two-column layout. Let's try the same thing with this design.

Figure 7-3: Consider how an image will be cropped for a header, and make sure it has a tight focus.
Source: Flickr.com © frostnova

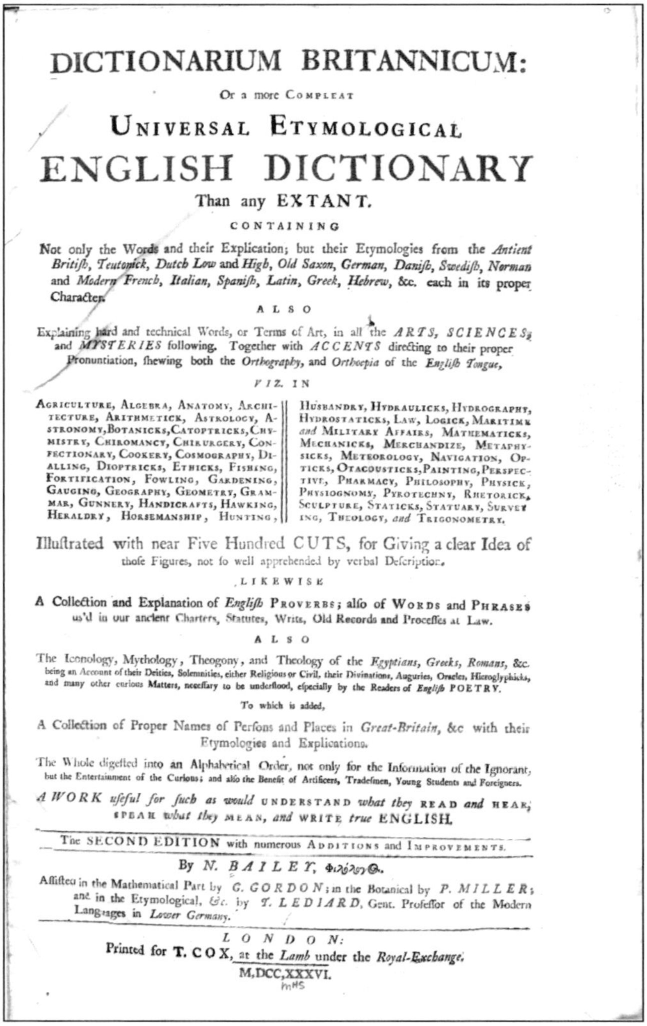

DICTIONARIUM BRITANNICUM:

Or a more COMPLEAT

UNIVERSAL ETYMOLOGICAL

ENGLISH DICTIONARY

Than any EXTANT.

CONTAINING

Not only the Words and their Explication; but their Etymologies from the *Antient Britiſh*, *Teutonick*, *Dutch Low* and *High*, *Old Saxon*, *German*, *Daniſh*, *Swediſh*, *Norman* and *Modern French*, *Italian*, *Spaniſh*, *Latin*, *Greek*, *Hebrew*, &c. each in its proper Character.

ALSO

Explaining hard and technical Words, or Terms of Art, in all the *ARTS*, *SCIENCES*, and *MYSTERIES* following. Together with *ACCENTS* directing to their proper Pronuntiation, ſhewing both the *Orthography*, and *Orthoepia* of the *Engliſh Tongue*,

VIZ. IN

AGRICULTURE, ALGEBRA, ANATOMY, ARCHITECTURE, ARITHMETICK, ASTROLOGY, ASTRONOMY, BOTANICKS, CATOPTRICKS, CHYMISTRY, CHIROMANCY, CHIRURGERY, CONFECTIONARY, COOKERY, COSMOGRAPHY, DIALLING, DIOPTRICKS, ETHICKS, FISHING, FORTIFICATION, FOWLING, GARDENING, GAUGING, GEOGRAPHY, GEOMETRY, GRAMMAR, GUNNERY, HANDICRAFTS, HAWKING, HERALDRY, HORSEMANSHIP, HUNTING, HUSBANDRY, HYDRAULICKS, HYDROGRAPHY, HYDROSTATICKS, LAW, LOGICK, MARITIME *and* MILITARY AFFAIRS, MATHEMATICKS, MECHANICKS, MERCHANDIZE, METAPHYSICKS, METEOROLOGY, NAVIGATION, OPTICKS, OTACOUSTICKS, PAINTING, PERSPECTIVE, PHARMACY, PHILOSOPHY, PHYSICK, PHYSIOGNOMY, PYROTECHNY, RHETORICK, SCULPTURE, STATICKS, STATUARY, SURVEYING, THEOLOGY, *and* TRIGONOMETRY.

Illuſtrated with near Five Hundred CUTS, for Giving a clear Idea of thoſe Figures, not ſo well apprehended by verbal Deſcription.

LIKEWISE

A Collection and Explanation of *Engliſh* PROVERBS; alſo of WORDS and PHRASES us'd in our ancient Charters, Statutes, Writs, Old Records and Proceſſes at Law.

ALSO

The Iconology, Mythology, Theogony, and Theology of the *Egyptians*, *Greeks*, *Romans*, &c. being an Account of their Deities, Solemnities, either Religious or Civil, their Divinations, Auguries, Oracles, Hieroglyphicks, and many other curious Matters, neceſſary to be underſtood, eſpecially by the Readers of *Engliſh* POETRY.

To which is added,

A Collection of Proper Names of Perſons and Places in *Great-Britain*, &c with their Etymologies and Explications.

The Whole digeſted into an Alphabetical Order, not only for the Information of the Ignorant, but the Entertainment of the Curious; and alſo the Benefit of Artificers, Tradeſmen, Young Students and Foreigners.

A WORK uſeful for ſuch as would UNDERSTAND *what they* READ *and* HEAR, SPEAK *what they* MEAN, *and* WRITE *true* ENGLISH.

The SECOND EDITION with numerous ADDITIONS and IMPROVEMENTS.

By *N. BAILEY*, Φιλόλογος.

Aſſiſted in the Mathematical Part by *G. GORDON*; in the Botanical by *P. MILLER*; and in the Etymological, &c. by *T. LEDIARD*, Gent. Profeſſor of the Modern Languages in *Lower Germany*.

LONDON:

Printed for T. COX, at the *Lamb* under the *Royal-Exchange*.

M,DCC,XXXVI.

Figure 7-4: Old books and other printed materials can be a great source of ideas for basic layout.
Source: fromoldbooks.org

Now that you have the most basic design elements of the site figured out, you can start considering some details for the design. Figure 7-5 has an interesting concrete texture, but with a geometric pattern included. It fits with the grungy mood perfectly.

The transparent glass panel in Figure 7-6 could easily be adapted to a design. Transparency effects are a common design element to begin with.

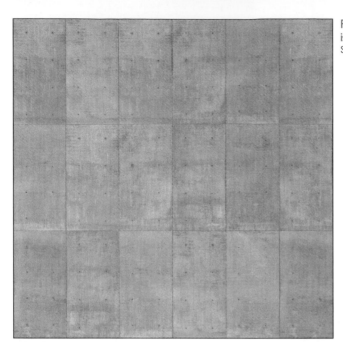

Figure 7-5: The mix of geometric pattern and organic texture is unexpected.
Source: Flickr.com © seier+seier

Figure 7-6: Transparent objects and elements are common in web design.
Source: Flickr.com © Casey Yancey

Let's find one more detail to incorporate into the design. Details can turn a design that's average into something great if used well, so don't overlook this part of the idea-generating process. Details can also be some of the easiest things to find in abstract sources of inspiration.

Figure 7-7 has a unique glowing shape. You can apply a glow effect to elements on the page to help them stand out, so let's grab this image for later ideas, too.

Now that you have your design elements, it's time to actually create the design.

Figure 7-7: This glowing effect is easily emulated in design.
Source: Flickr.com © Yohan Creemers

ADAPTING ELEMENTS

Grab the color scheme to start with. Taking the flower image, you can grab a couple of sample colors from it and then build from there. Figure 7-8 shows what I came up with.

The header design will come first. Take the image selected for the header and colorize it so it fits with the color scheme. You could add a gradient overlay and some grunge effects, too, so that it fits the mood of the site. Figure 7-9 shows what that will look like.

Next comes the background for the main content area. You can use the gray from the color scheme, and the geometric-patterned concrete texture. Figure 7-10 shows this texture.

Figure 7-8: Website color scheme.

Figure 7-9: Website header.
Source: Flickr.com © frostnova

Figure 7-10: Background texture based on concrete image.

Instead of the rectangles in the original image, I've opted for diamonds. It's more visually interesting, while keeping the same feeling.

From there, you'll need to add the content. You can use the book page layout of one column, two columns, and then one column. See Figure 7-11.

Figure 7-11: The main content layout, based on the book page.

That's a good start, although maybe a little plain. So let's add some of the details, like the transparency and glow effects. Let's add these around the "Coming Soon!" section, since you'll want this to stand out. See Figure 7-12.

You can also add some glow effects around the typography in the header, to make it stand out from the background, as shown in Figure 7-13.

The final result is shown in Figure 7-14.

COMING SOON!

A wonderful serenity has taken possession of my entire soul, like these sweet mornings of spring which I enjoy with my whole heart. I am alone, and feel the charm of existence in this spot, which was created for the bliss of souls like mine. I am so happy, my dear friend, so absorbed in the exquisite sense of mere tranquil existence, that I neglect my talents. I should be incapable of drawing a single stroke at the present moment; and yet I feel that I never was a greater artist than now.

Latest on the Blog

Far far away, behind the word mountains, far from the countries Vokalia and Consonantia, there live the blind texts. Separated they live in Bookmarksgrove right at the coast of the Semantics, a large language ocean. A small river named Duden flows by their place and supplies it with the necessary regelialia. It is a paradisematic country, in which roasted parts of sentences fly into your mouth.

Read An Excerpt

Even the all-powerful Pointing has no control about the blind texts it is an almost unorthographic life One day however a small line of blind text by the name of Lorem Ipsum decided to leave for the far World of Grammar. The Big Oxmox advised her not to do so, because there were thousands of bad Commas, wild Question Marks and devious Semikoli, but the Little Blind Text didn't listen.

Figure 7-12: A transparent background and glowing border set featured content apart.

Figure 7-13: More glow effects in the header design.

Figure 7-14: The final result!

Notice there's a navigation bar under the header, with one of the colors from the color scheme. The typography on the page is also based on the colors of the original color scheme, just in a darker shade.

CONCLUSION

In the real world, you'll likely draw inspiration from both direct and abstract sources for the same project. In some cases, you might even base an entire design around a single abstract image. As has already been mentioned, using only a single source of abstract inspiration can be a perfectly legitimate way to design a site, though you'll want to avoid that with direct inspiration.

Learning to process ideas as you see them in your surroundings is a valuable skill for any designer to have. Then, when you're ready to sit down and start a project, you'll already have a wealth of ideas ready for you.

The key thing to remember when designing based on the work of others is to make sure your designs are uniquely yours, despite the origin of their parts. If you spend the time to consider how others have solved the challenges you face in your own projects, and then apply not just the individual elements, but also the reasoning *behind* those elements, you'll have a much stronger design in the end.

FINDING INSPIRATION IN EVERYDAY LIFE

EVERYWHERE YOU TURN, potential sources of ideas surround you. Whether in your home or office, or traveling somewhere exotic, there's almost certainly something you could adapt into a design. All it takes is learning to look at things the right way.

I live in northern New England, in a rural area. And yet there are things around me on a daily basis that I can draw inspiration from. All I have to do is look for them. One way I do that is to carry a camera with me all the time. (My smartphone has an excellent built-in camera, so even if I'm not carrying my DSLR, I have a camera with me. You can tell which ones are smartphone images based on the filters applied to them.) I take pictures of just about everything.

So here's a sampling of photos I've taken during the past year, and some commentary on how you might adapt them into a website design. These are all just photos of the things that surround me on a daily basis, and weren't taken with this project specifically in mind.

Figure 8-1: Color scheme: white and brown. Texture: sand, shell. Negative space: the expanse of sand around the shell. Basic layout: asymmetrical.

Figure 8-2: Mood: dark and dingy. Details: reflections.

Figure 8-3: Feeling: vintage. Color scheme: shades of greenish-blue. Textures: wood, grass.

Figure 8-4: Color scheme: purples and greens. Texture: wood grain.

Figure 8-6: Color scheme: sea green, brown, black. Texture: wood grain. Details: translucency, bubbles.

Figure 8-5: Mood: hopeful. Color scheme: grays and blues. Details: light flares.

Figure 8-7: Color scheme: greens. Mood: clean and fresh.

Figure 8-8: Mood: dark and sinister. Layout: balance of negative/positive space, depth. Details: vignetting.

Figure 8-9: Color scheme: yellows, blues, greens, and purples.
Details: light flares.

Figure 8-10: Mood: Dark and formal. Textures: stone.
Color scheme: dark gray with bright red accents.
Details: classical columns, stone pattern.

Figure 8-11: Color scheme: muted browns and creams. Details: reflections, transparency. Shape: curves.

Figure 8-12: Mood: grungy. Color scheme: brown, purple, red, cream. Textures: wood grain, skin.

Figure 8-13: Color scheme: yellow, black, brown.
Textures: wood grain, smooth and glossy.
Details: reflections. Shape: curves.

Figure 8-14: Color scheme: yellow, black, and red.
Details: vignetting.

Figure 8-15: Mood: light and airy. Color scheme: white, grays, pink, and peach. Negative space: in the sky.

Figure 8-16: Mood: bright and cheerful. Color scheme: blues, white, and red.

Figure 8-17: Mood: natural and bright. Color scheme: blues, gold, green. Basic layout: large minimalist header, darker content area, bright footer, also depth.

Figure 8-18: Color scheme: blues, muted green, and black. Textures: denim, felted wool. Negative space: lots of black.

Figure 8-19: Mood: dark but colorful. Details: bokeh pattern.

Figure 8-21: Color scheme: blue-green, blues, brown, cream. Shapes: triangles in the bridge railings.

Figure 8-20: Color scheme: black, blues. Textures: wispy clouds.

Figure 8-22: Mood: dark and futuristic. Details: light flare.

Figure 8-23: Mood: formal. Shapes: both organic and geometric shapes, and the contrast between the two. Textures: brick.

Figure 8-24: Mood: subdued. Textures: water. Basic layout: light header, dark body content, lighter footer. Shape: organic shapes of the mountains.

Figure 8-25: Mood: grungy but bright. Textures: fabric, fur. Patterns: stripes and plaid. Contrast: color vs. black and white.

Figure 8-26: Mood: subdued and surreal. Color scheme: blues, grays, creams, and white. Textures: snow.

Figure 8-27: Color scheme: shades of blue. Texture: crystals. Shapes: hard lines.

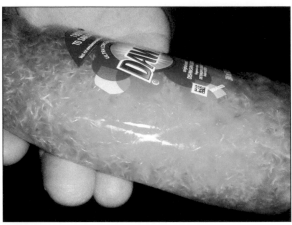

Figure 8-28: Mood: dark and dreary. Details: red lights. Color scheme: muted browns and greens with red accents.

Figure 8-29: Mood: bright and cheerful. Color scheme: red, blue and black. Details: typography.

Figure 8-30: Patterns: stripes in the house siding. Textures: wood grain, grass.

Figure 8-31: Color scheme: purples, peaches, and green. Basic layout: light header, darker body.

Figure 8-32: Mood: dark. Color scheme: dark greens with white and bright orange accents.

Figure 8-33: Color scheme: muted red, white, and green. Patterns: diamond brickwork.

Figure 8-34: Mood: bright. Color scheme: golds and greens.

Figure 8-35: Patterns: stripes. Shape: curves.

Figure 8-36: Mood: dark and industrial, vintage. Color scheme: bright, red and gray.

Figure 8-37: Mood: bright. Color scheme: green, red, gray, and blue. Textures: wood grain.

Figure 8-38: Negative space: in the spider web. Details: spider web.

Figure 8-39: Mood: stark and colorful. Color scheme: bright gold, reds. Layout: depth and focusing attention.

Figure 8-40: Mood: peaceful. Color scheme: muted blues and grays, bright greens.

Figure 8-41: Mood: clean and fresh, inviting.

Figure 8-42: Mood: creepy and grungy. Color scheme: muted greens and tans, gray.

Figure 8-43: Mood: bright and happy. Color scheme: bright blues and bright greens.

Figure 8-44: Basic layout: asymmetrical columns with a light header. Details: perspective lines.

Figure 8-45: Mood: antique. Textures: brick. Details: typography.

Figure 8-46: Mood: subdued. Color scheme: white, grays, tans, and muted pinks. Textures: bark. Pattern: lines.

Figure 8-47: Color scheme: shades of gray. Textures: chrome and metal, mesh.

Figure 8-48: Mood: grungy and light. Textures: stone, rust. Details: vintage typography.

Figure 8-49: Color scheme: white, tan, bright blue. Textures: fluffy vegetation.

All the images in this chapter have one thing in common: they're a part of my everyday life. I didn't have to go seeking out inspiration; it came to me. By carrying a camera with me, I'm ready whenever I see something that might offer up ideas at a later date. Whether you spend time on a daily basis taking pictures of things or go out specifically for each project, don't overlook your daily surroundings when it comes to finding ideas.

Index